NOSTALGIC TRIVIA FOR SENIORS

CHERISH YOUR GOLDEN MEMORIES FROM THE

1950S TO 1990S!

IMPRINT

1st edition

ISBN: 9791282240420

CONTACT

TG Edition
Thomas Larch
Ritterweg 16C
39010 St. Martin in Passeier
Italy
E-mail: support@tg-edition.com

IMAGE REFERENCES
freepik

DISCLAIMER

All information, instructions and strategies contained in this book are used at your own risk. The author cannot be held liable for any damages of any kind for any legal reason.

For damages of a material or non-material nature caused by the use or non-use of the information or use of incorrect and/or incomplete information, any liability claims against the author are excluded. Any legal claims and claims for damages are therefore also excluded. This work has been compiled and written down with the utmost care. However, the author does not assume any liability for the topicality, completeness and quality of the information. Misprints and incorrect information cannot be completely ruled out.

No legal responsibility or liability in any form whatsoever can be accepted for incorrect indications.

COPYRIGHT

READY FOR

EVEN MORE NOSTALGIC FUN?

Unwind with **10 nostalgic word search puzzles** that relax your mind, spark memories, and celebrate the good old days.

Scan the QR code

to download your puzzles for free!

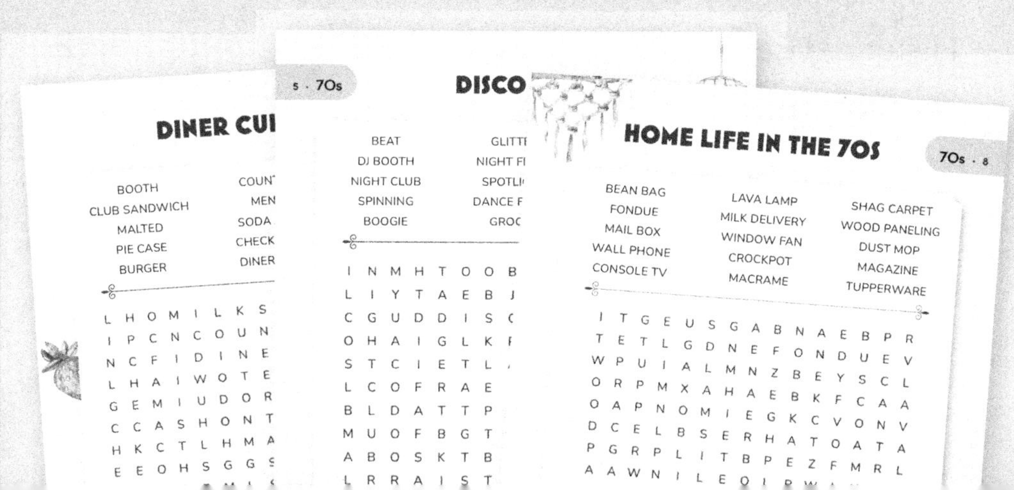

CONTENT

CHAPTER THREE
The 1970s

CHAPTER FOUR
The 1980s

CHAPTER FIVE
The 1990s

ANSWER KEY

WELCOME TO

NOSTALGIC TRIVIA FOR SENIORS!

Picture this: You're sitting around the table with **old friends**, **sharing stories** and **laughing** about all of the wild hairstyles, the **classic tunes**, and the **unforgettable moments** from "**back in the day**." Someone hums a tune from the '60s, another recalls their first color television set, and before you know it, the room is alive with **memories**. That's exactly what this book is all about. It's your chance to **stroll down memory lane** with a smile on your face and **have a few good laughs** along the way!

Whether you grew up in the **rockin' '50s**, the **groovy '60s**, the **disco-fueled '70s**, the **neon-lit '80s**, or the **pop-culture-packed '90s**, this book is your ticket to **reliving the moments** that made all of those decades special.

We've packed this book with **500 trivia questions** covering everything from **daily life**, **entertainment**, and

history to the biggest **technological breakthroughs** and **sports achievements**. Along the way, you'll find **fun facts**, **conversation starters**, and even some **space to jot down your favorite memories** because, let's be honest, you've got some amazing stories that are just waiting to be told!

So, grab your favorite chair, maybe a cup of coffee (or a milkshake if you're feeling nostalgic), and let's get started!

HOW TO ENJOY THIS BOOK

This book is way more than just a trivia challenge. It's a **memory booster**, a **conversation starter**, and a whole lot of **fun** rolled into one!

Here's how you can make the most of it:

If you're flying **solo**, this book is perfect for **keeping your mind sharp** and **your memories fresh**. Challenge yourself by **answering the trivia questions**, then flip to the answer section to see how well you did. Did you ace it? If so, give yourself a pat on the back! Got stumped on a few? No worries—that just means you'll have even more fun rediscovering those facts!

You can also use the **reflection prompts** to **jot down your memories**. What was your favorite childhood snack? Who was your biggest celebrity crush in the '70s? The best part? **There are no wrong answers**; it's your chance to **relive the good times** and make a **mini-memoir for future generations** to enjoy!

This book also shines when you share it **with others**! Whether it's at a **family gathering** or a **game night** with friends, you can use these questions to **share all of your golden memories**, start up **fun conversations**, learn interesting **unknown facts** about others, or even turn these questions into a **fun competition**!

Here are a few ways you can challenge others:

Trivia Battle: Take turns reading questions and see who gets the most right.

Memory Lane Challenge: Instead of just answering, share a story related to the question. For example, if a question asks about drive-in theaters, tell everyone about the first movie you saw at one!

Team Play: Split into groups and keep score for some friendly competition.

No matter how you choose to enjoy it, this book is here to **bring back** all of those **wonderful memories**, **spark up** some great **conversations**, and maybe even **teach you a thing or two** (because, hey, even the best of us forget a detail or two over time!).

So, are you ready to take a trip through the decades? Let's get started—a whole world of nostalgia is waiting for you!

CHAPTER ONE

The 1950s

Let's step back to the fabulous '50s, where **poodle skirts** twirled, **jukeboxes** ruled, and the **King of Rock 'n' Roll** made history! This was the decade when **sock hops** were the place to be, and if you weren't cruising in a **Chevy Bel Air**, were you even cool?

The airwaves were on fire with hits from **Elvis Presley**, whose „Hound Dog" had everyone swinging their hips. Meanwhile, **Buddy Holly** was melting hearts with „Peggy Sue," and **Little Richard** shouted „Tutti Frutti" like there was no tomorrow. And let's not forget the sweet harmonies of **The Platters**, who had us slow dancing to „Only You." If you were lucky, you might have caught a **doo-wop group** harmonizing on the street corner while you sipped a **chocolate malt** at the local soda shop.

Television was becoming the centerpiece of the living room, and families gathered around to watch **I Love Lucy** and **The Ed Sullivan Show**. Life was simpler, yet oh-so-exciting, as America stepped into the golden age of **rock 'n' roll**, **drive-in movies**, and the birth of **teen culture**.

Go slip on your saddle shoes and get ready to test your '50s know-how! Let's see if you can still jive with the best of them!

Daily Life & Childhood Memories

1. What was a common way kids listened to their favorite music in the 1950s?

a) Cassette tapes
b) Vinyl records
c) Eight Tracks
d) MP3 players

2. Which popular doll was first introduced in 1959?

a) Raggedy Ann
b) G.I. Joe
c) Barbie
d) Cabbage Patch Kids

3. What was the most popular soft drink in the 1950s?

a) Pepsi
b) Coca-Cola
c) Dr Pepper
d) Sprite

4. What was a favorite after-school TV show for kids in the 1950s?

a) Mister Rogers' Neighborhood
b) The Mickey Mouse Club
c) Sesame Street
d) Blue's Clues

5. What hairstyle was iconic for young girls in the 1950s?

a) Pixie cut
b) Poodle cut
c) Mohawk
d) Beehive

6. The first Barbie doll was released in 1953.

a) True
b) False

7. What was the name of the popular detergent that promised to make clothes „whiter than white" in the 1950s?

a) Tide
b) Duz
c) Oxydol
d) Rinso

8. Which popular home appliance saw a major boom in sales in the 1950s, revolutionizing meal preparation?

a) Refrigerator
b) Electric blender
c) Pressure cooker
d) Dishwasher

9. What was a common way to keep milk cold before modern refrigerators became standard in every home?

a) Iceboxes
b) Wooden coolers
c) Underground storage
d) Ceramic jugs

10. Which of the following was a popular board game first introduced in the 1950s?

a) Clue
b) Candy Land
c) Risk
d) Life

11. What was the name of the fabric that became a fashion staple due to its wrinkle-resistant properties?

a) Nylon
b) Polyester
c) Dacron
d) Rayon

DID YOU KNOW?

In 1950, the **Diners Club card** became the **world's first credit card**, revolutionizing how people paid for things. Before this, most transactions were done with cash, checks, or store-specific credit lines. The idea of carrying around a little piece of plastic to buy dinner was a completely new concept!

12. Which company released the first mass-produced color television set in 1954?

a) General Electric
b) RCA
c) Zenith
d) Philco

13. Which breakfast cereal, first introduced in the 1950s, became a major hit with kids?

a) Trix
b) Corn Pops
c) Cheerios
d) Cocoa Puffs

14. What was the main fuel source used in most American home kitchens during the early 1950s?

a) Coal
b) Gas
c) Electricity
d) Kerosene

15. The 1950s saw a boom in which type of frozen food, making meal preparation a whole lot easier for busy families?

a) Pizza
b) TV dinners
c) Frozen fruit bars
d) Fish sticks

16. What was a common classroom punishment for students who misbehaved in the 1950s?

a) Writing lines on the chalkboard
b) Detention
c) Suspension
d) A verbal warning

17. Which type of bicycle was most popular in the 1950s?

a) Cruiser bike
b) BMX bike
c) Road bike
d) Folding bike

18. What was the name of the inexpensive rubbery plastic material kids could mold, shape, and copy newspaper print?

a) Shrinky Dinks
b) Silly Putty
c) Play-Doh
d) Plastigoop

19. Which outdoor game, often played in the street, was popular with kids in the 1950s?

a) Jacks
b) Stickball
c) Marbles
d) All of the above

20. What was a common feature in many American homes in the 1950s, popular for storing leftovers?

a) Tupperware
b) Mason jars
c) Ice trays
d) Breadboxes

Entertainment & Culture

1. Which television show made history by featuring a real-life interracial couple as its lead characters, breaking barriers in 1950s entertainment?

a) The Ed Sullivan Show
b) I Love Lucy
c) The Twilight Zone
d) Your Show of Shows

2. What famous film featured the iconic phrase, „Here's looking at you, kid"?

a) Casablanca
b) Rebel Without a Cause
c) Sunset Boulevard
d) Roman Holiday

3. What color were poodle skirts typically associated with?

a) Pink
b) Green
c) Blue
d) Red

4. What was the first major animated feature film released by Disney in the 1950s?

a) Sleeping Beauty
b) Peter Pan
c) Cinderella
d) Alice in Wonderland

5. What book by J.D. Salinger became a defining novel of teenage angst?

a) Lord of the Flies
b) Catcher in the Rye
c) On the Road
d) Fahrenheit 451

6. Who starred alongside James Dean in Rebel Without a Cause?

a) Audrey Hepburn
b) Natalie Wood
c) Marilyn Monroe
d) Grace Kelly

7. Which iconic TV family lived at 485 Mapleton Drive?

a) The Nelsons
b) The Cleavers
c) The Flintstones
d) The Ricardos

DID YOU KNOW?

Television exploded in popularity during the 1950s. In 1950, only 9% of American households owned a TV, but by the end of the decade, that number had skyrocketed to **90%**! Families gathered around their sets to watch classics like **I Love Lucy, The Twilight Zone**, and **The Ed Sullivan Show**.

8. What kind of shoes were known as „blue suede shoes," made famous by Elvis Presley?

a) Penny loafers
b) Saddle shoes
c) Moccasins
d) Suede loafers

9. What was the name of the first successful 3D movie, released in 1952?

a) House of Wax
b) The Creature from the Black Lagoon
c) Dial M for Murder
d) Bwana Devil

10. What phrase, popularized in the 1950s, was used to describe someone very cool?

a) „Far out"
b) „Neat-o"
c) „Hip to the jive"
d) „Groovy"

11. I Love Lucy was the first TV show filmed in front of a live studio audience.

a) True
b) False

12. Who played the Lone Ranger in the popular 1950s TV series?

a) Clayton Moore
b) Roy Rogers
c) Gene Autry
d) Hopalong Cassidy

13. What was the name of the spaceship in the 1956 sci-fi film Forbidden Planet?

a) Enterprise
b) Discovery One
c) C-57D
d) Nostromo

14. What actor starred in The Ten Commandments, one of the biggest movies of the 1950s?

a) Gregory Peck
b) Kirk Douglas
c) Charlton Heston
d) Burt Lancaster

15. James Dean won an Oscar during his lifetime.

a) True
b) False

16. What was the first sitcom to feature an African American lead character?

a) The Amos 'n' Andy Show
b) Leave It to Beaver
c) Father Knows Best
d) The Honeymooners

17. Who sang the 1958 hit song Johnny B. Goode?

a) Elvis Presley
b) Chuck Berry
c) Buddy Holly
d) Little Richard

18. **What iconic theme park opened in 1955?**

a) Universal Studios
b) Six Flags
c) Disneyland
d) Knott's Berry Farm

19. **What was the highest-grossing movie of the 1950s?**

a) Ben-Hur
b) The Bridge on the River Kwai
c) The Ten Commandments
d) Singin' in the Rain

20. **Which 1950s rock 'n' roll legend tragically died in a plane crash in 1959?**

a) Chuck Berry
b) Buddy Holly
c) Jerry Lee Lewis
d) Ritchie Valens

Historical Events & Headlines

1. What major conflict began in 1950 and lasted until 1953?

a) Vietnam War
b) Korean War
c) Gulf War
d) Cuban Revolution

2. Who was elected as U.S. President in 1952?

a) Harry S. Truman
b) Dwight D. Eisenhower
c) John F. Kennedy
d) Richard Nixon

3. In 1957, the Soviet Union launched the first artificial satellite into space. What was its name?

a) Luna 1
b) Sputnik 1
c) Vostok
d) Explorer 1

4. The Civil Rights Act was signed into law in the 1950s.

a) True
b) False

5. Which international treaty organization was founded in 1955 to counter NATO?

a) Warsaw Pact
b) United Nations
c) SEATO
d) OPEC

6. What famous American landmark was completed in 1959?

a) Mount Rushmore
b) The Gateway Arch
c) The Space Needle
d) Hawaii's Statehood

7. What medical breakthrough did Dr. Jonas Salk develop in the 1950s?

a) Polio vaccine
b) Penicillin
c) Chemotherapy
d) Insulin therapy

8. Which 1950s event heightened Cold War tensions between the U.S. and the Soviet Union?

a) Bay of Pigs Invasion
b) Cuban Missile Crisis
c) U-2 Spy Plane Incident
d) The Berlin Airlift

9. What was the landmark Supreme Court decision in 1954 that ruled segregation in public schools unconstitutional?

a) Roe v. Wade
b) Plessy v. Ferguson
c) Brown v. Board of Education
d) Miranda v. Arizona

10. Alaska became a U.S. state before Hawaii.

a) True
b) False

11. What organization was created in 1958 to advance U.S. space exploration?

a) NOAA
b) NASA
c) CIA
d) NORAD

12. In what year did Queen Elizabeth II ascend to the British throne?

a) 1950
b) 1952
c) 1955
d) 1957

13. What country underwent a revolution in 1959, leading to a new Communist government?

a) China
b) Vietnam
c) Cuba
d) North Korea

14. What U.S. holiday was officially established in 1954, replacing Armistice Day?

a) Labor Day
b) Memorial Day
c) Veterans Day
d) Independence Day

DID YOU KNOW?

The **birth of rock 'n' roll** came in **1955** when **Rock Around the Clock by Bill Haley & His Comets** became a smash hit. This song marked the beginning of a **music revolution** that would bring **Elvis Presley**, **Chuck Berry**, and **Buddy Holly** into the spotlight.

15. The European Economic Community (EEC), a precursor to the European Union, was established in the 1950s.

a) True
b) False

16. What civil rights leader famously refused to give up her bus seat in Montgomery, Alabama, in 1955?

a) Rosa Parks
b) Coretta Scott King
c) Shirley Chisholm
d) Ella Baker

17. The „Kitchen Debate“ of 1959 was a famous exchange between Richard Nixon and which Soviet leader?

a) Joseph Stalin
b) Leonid Brezhnev
c) Nikita Khrushchev
d) Mikhail Gorbachev

18. In 1953, which mountain was successfully climbed for the first time?

a) Mount Kilimanjaro
b) Mount McKinley
c) Mount Everest
d) Mount Fuji

19. What was the name of the major nuclear test series conducted by the U.S. in the 1950s?

a) Operation Crossroads
b) Operation Ivy
c) Operation Castle
d) Operation Plumbbob

20. The first successful organ transplant was performed in the 1950s.

a) True
b) False

Technology & Innovation

1. What was the first credit card introduced in the 1950s?

a) Visa
b) Mastercard
c) American Express
d) Diners Club

2. What major medical device, widely used today, was first successfully tested in the 1950s?

a) Pacemaker
b) MRI scanner
c) Insulin pump
d) Cochlear implant

3. The first color television broadcast in the U.S. occurred in 1951.

a) True
b) False

4. What type of nuclear technology became widely developed and tested in the 1950s?

a) Nuclear fission
b) Nuclear fusion
c) Cold fusion
d) Thorium reactors

5. What major car safety feature was introduced by Volvo in 1959?

a) Seat belts
b) Airbags
c) Anti-lock brakes
d) Crumple zones

6. Which 1950s invention allowed people to cook food much faster than traditional ovens?

a) Toaster oven
b) Microwave oven
c) Convection oven
d) Induction stove

7. The first successful commercial jet airliner, introduced in 1952, was called what?

a) Boeing 747
b) Concorde
c) De Havilland Comet
d) Douglas DC-8

8. What electronic device, invented in the 1950s, helped revolutionize computers?

a) Transistor
b) Vacuum tube
c) Microchip
d) Diode

9. The first satellite successfully sent into space was launched by the United States.

a) True
b) False

10. What company released the first mass-produced electric guitar in the 1950s?

a) Gibson
b) Fender
c) Gretsch
d) Rickenbacker

DID YOU KNOW?

Going to the movies was a completely different experience in the 1950s. By 1958, there were **over 4,000 drive-in movie theaters** across the U.S., making them the ultimate hangout spot for teenagers and couples. With a car full of friends and a giant tub of popcorn, a Friday night at the drive-in was a must!

11. What was the name of the first intercontinental ballistic missile (ICBM) developed in the 1950s?

a) Minuteman
b) Titan II
c) Atlas
d) Redstone

12. What widely used household appliance was introduced by Whirlpool in the 1950s?

a) Dishwasher
b) Refrigerator with automatic defrost
c) Clothes dryer
d) Electric stove

13. What scientific theory was first widely accepted in the 1950s, revolutionizing the study of geology?

a) Plate tectonics
b) Relativity
c) Quantum mechanics
d) Evolution

14. The first video game was invented in the 1950s.

a) True
b) False

15. What was the name of the first mass-produced car to feature a V8 engine?

a) Ford Mustang
b) Chevrolet Bel Air
c) Oldsmobile Rocket 88
d) Pontiac GTO

16. What communication technology saw significant advancements in the 1950s, making long-distance calls easier?

a) Telegraph
b) Satellite communication
c) Transatlantic telephone cable
d) Fiber optics

17. The first man-made object to reach the Moon was launched in the 1950s.

a) True
b) False

18. What was the most common method of home entertainment that became widely available in the 1950s?

a) Radio
b) Television
c) Home movie projectors
d) Phonographs

19. Which company introduced the first mass-market transistor radio in the 1950s?

a) Sony
b) RCA
c) Zenith
d) Motorola

20. What major breakthrough in medical imaging was first developed in the 1950s?

a) X-ray imaging
b) Ultrasound
c) MRI
d) CT scan

Sports & Big Achievements

1. Which baseball team won the World Series in 1955, marking their first championship victory?

a) New York Yankees
b) Brooklyn Dodgers
c) Chicago White Sox
d) St. Louis Cardinals

2. Who was the heavyweight boxing champion for most of the 1950s?

a) Joe Louis
b) Sonny Liston
c) Rocky Marciano
d) Floyd Patterson

3. The first official NBA All-Star Game was played in 1951.

a) True
b) False

4. What major motorsport event, first held in 1950, became the premier global racing championship?

a) Le Mans 24 Hours
b) Formula One World Championship
c) Indianapolis 500
d) Monaco Grand Prix

5. In 1954, Roger Bannister became the first person to do what in athletics?

a) Run a sub-4-minute mile
b) Jump over 8 feet in the high jump
c) Break the 10-second barrier in the 100m
d) Throw a javelin over 100m

6. Which country hosted the 1952 Summer Olympics?

a) Australia
b) Sweden
c) Finland
d) Canada

7. Who won the most Grand Slam singles titles in men's tennis during the 1950s?

a) Ken Rosewall
b) Rod Laver
c) Roy Emerson
d) Frank Sedgman

8. The Baltimore Colts won their first NFL Championship in 1958 in what is often called „The Greatest Game Ever Played."

a) True
b) False

9. Which golf legend won his first Masters Tournament in 1958?

a) Jack Nicklaus
b) Ben Hogan
c) Sam Snead
d) Arnold Palmer

10. What historic event occurred at the 1956 Melbourne Olympics involving several countries withdrawing in protest?

a) Soviet invasion of Hungary
b) Apartheid policies of South Africa
c) Boycott over nuclear testing
d) Political disputes in the Middle East

11. Which team won the 1957 NBA Championship, marking their first title?

a) Minneapolis Lakers
b) St. Louis Hawks
c) Boston Celtics
d) Philadelphia Warriors

12. **The first televised college football game was broadcast in the 1950s.**

a) True
b) False

13. **Who was the first African American to win a tennis Grand Slam title, achieving this in 1956?**

a) Arthur Ashe
b) Althea Gibson
c) Charlie Pasarell
d) Yannick Noah

DID YOU KNOW?

One of the biggest toy crazes of the decade was the **Hula Hoop**, introduced in **1958**. In just **four months**, an astonishing **25 million hoops** were sold! Kids, teens, and even adults got in on the fun, trying to master the art of keeping the hoop spinning.

14. In 1950, which horse won the first-ever Horse of the Year Award?

a) Seabiscuit
b) Citation
c) Swaps
d) Native Dancer

15. How many World Series titles did the New York Yankees win during the 1950s?

a) 3
b) 5
c) 7
d) 9

16. Which basketball player was named NBA MVP three times during the 1950s?

a) Bill Russell
b) Bob Cousy
c) George Mikan
d) Dolph Schayes

17. The first FIFA World Cup held after World War II took place in 1954.

a) True
b) False

18. In 1951, which historic boxing match became the first-ever to be broadcast coast-to-coast on national television, changing the way fans experienced the sport?

a) Sugar Ray Robinson vs. Jake LaMotta VI
b) Rocky Marciano vs. Joe Louis
c) Jersey Joe Walcott vs. Ezzard Charles
d) Archie Moore vs. Harold Johnson

19. Which team won the Stanley Cup the most times in the 1950s?

a) Toronto Maple Leafs
b) Detroit Red Wings
c) Montreal Canadiens
d) Boston Bruins

20. Who was the first woman to win five U.S. Figure Skating Championships in a row during the 1950s?

a) Peggy Fleming
b) Tenley Albright
c) Carol Heiss
d) Dorothy Hamill

REMEMBERING THE FABULOUS '50s!

The 1950s were a time of **jukebox hits**, **soda fountains**, and the golden age of **television**. It was the decade that gave us **rock 'n' roll**, **drive-in movies**, and some of the most **iconic cars** ever made. Did you know that in 1955, there were over 7,000 drive-in theaters across the U.S.? Whether you were dancing to **Elvis**, tuning in to **I Love Lucy**, or sipping a **milkshake** at the local diner, the '50s had a little something for everyone.

Let's take a trip down memory lane and relive some of the moments that made this decade unforgettable!

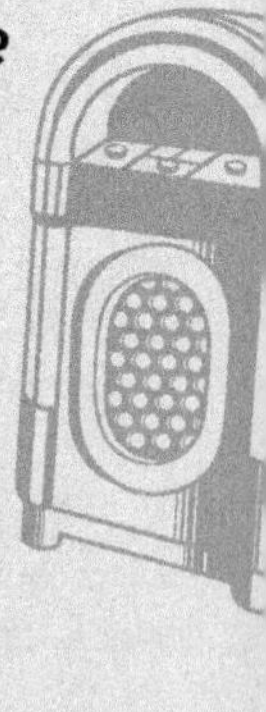

Talk & Think About the 1950s

Use these fun questions to relive old memories, share your favorite stories, or spark up a conversation with loved ones!

1. What is one of your favorite memories from the 1950s? A special event, a favorite toy, or maybe a family tradition?

2. What was your go-to song in the 1950s? Did you dance to Elvis, swoon over Frank Sinatra, or tap your feet to Chuck Berry?

3. Think back to your childhood home—what did your kitchen look like? What meals bring back the best memories?

4. Did you have a favorite TV show that you never missed? (I Love Lucy, The Twilight Zone, Leave It to Beaver—which one had you glued to the screen?)

5. What is your favorite fashion trend from the '50s? Poodle skirts, saddle shoes, or maybe the leather jacket like James Dean wore?

6. If you could go back and relive one day in the 1950s, which day would it be and why?

7. Did you earn any pocket money in the 1950s? What did you do, and how much did you earn?

8. Share a story about your family car from the 1950s—was it a beauty, a beater, or something in between?

9. What games or activities did you and your friends enjoy the most? Were you a hopscotch champion, a baseball slugger, or the neighborhood king of marbles?

10. How did you and your family spend weekends? Was it drive-in movies, picnics, or Sunday dinners around the table?

Write About the 1950s

Take a moment to jot down some of your favorite '50s memories. Maybe it was that unforgettable summer at the beach, your first big school dance, or the excitement of zooming down the street in your very first car.

Whatever it is, this is your chance to capture those golden moments and share them with family and friends.

The '50s were an era of joy, change, and rock 'n' roll— so let's keep the memories alive!

CHAPTER TWO

The 1960s

The 1960s were **bold**, **rebellious**, and **full of change**! It was the decade of **rock 'n' roll**, **space travel**, and **tie-dye** everything. If the '50s laid the foundation for **modern pop culture**, the '60s set it on fire! This was the era when **the Beatles** took over the world, **bell-bottoms** became the fashion statement of choice, and **color television** brought everything to life in vibrant detail.

It was a time when music wasn't just entertainment—it was a movement. Elvis may have ruled the '50s, but the '60s gave us the **British Invasion**, **Motown magic**, and the electrifying energy of **Woodstock**. From the smooth vocals of **The Supremes** (Baby Love) to the poetic genius of **Bob Dylan** (Blowin' in the Wind), music was the soundtrack to a decade of transformation. **The Beatles** made us want to Twist and Shout, while **The Rolling Stones** encouraged us to get (I Can't Get No) Satisfaction. **Aretha Franklin** demanded Respect, and **Marvin Gaye** asked What's Going On as social change swept the nation. And, of course, no list of '60s hits would be complete without **Jimi Hendrix** setting the stage on fire (both literally and figuratively) at Woodstock with Purple Haze.

But the '60s weren't just groovy tunes and psychedelic colors. It was also a decade of **incredible achievements**. In **1969**, the world held its breath as **Neil Armstrong** took his famous **first steps on the moon**, proving that "one small step for man" could mean a giant leap for all of humanity. Meanwhile, **cars got faster**, **movies got bolder**, and **television** brought us classics like **The Andy Griffith Show**, **Star Trek**, and **Laugh-In**.

Fashion was **louder**, **bolder**, and more **experimental** than ever. Goodbye poodle skirts, hello **go-go boots**! And let's not forget about the **slang**. If something was "**far out**" or "**outta sight**," you knew it was worth talking about!

Whether you were **twisting** the night away, **debating world events**, or just enjoying an ice-cold bottle of **Coca-Cola** while watching the latest episode of **Bonanza**, the 1960s were a decade that left an unforgettable mark on history.

So dust off your vinyl records, grab a seat, and get ready to relive the moments that made the '60s one of the most exciting decades of all time!

Daily Life & Childhood Memories

1. What popular toy, introduced in the 1960s, let kids make colorful, rubbery insects by heating liquid plastic?

a) Play-Doh
b) Shrinky Dinks
c) Creepy Crawlers
d) Etch A Sketch

2. Which TV show featuring a talking horse became a hit among children in the 1960s?

a) Flipper
b) Mr. Ed
c) Lassie
d) Dennis the Menace

3. What type of fabric became a staple in household items and clothing due to its durability and wrinkle resistance?

a) Nylon
b) Polyester
c) Rayon
d) Corduroy

4. What kind of dress, made famous by Mary Quant, became a fashion statement in the 1960s?

a) Shift dress
b) Maxi dress
c) Mini skirt
d) A-line dress

5. Which sugary breakfast cereal, first introduced in the 1960s, featured a pirate mascot?

a) Cocoa Puffs
b) Cap'n Crunch
c) Froot Loops
d) Lucky Charms

6. What household device, introduced in the 1960s, became an essential tool for home entertainment?

a) 8-track tape player
b) Home stereo system
c) Cassette tape recorder
d) Color television

7. What chewy fruit-flavored candy, originally called Opal Fruits, was introduced in the 1960s?

a) Skittles
b) Starburst
c) Jolly Rancher
d) Now and Later

8. Most kids in the 1960s wore bicycle helmets when riding their bikes.

a) True
b) False

9. What popular board game, released in 1965, required players to place plastic body parts on a cartoonish patient?

a) Life
b) Trouble
c) Operation
d) Twister

10. What fashionable hat, popular among both men and women, was commonly worn in the early 1960s?

a) Fedora
b) Beret
c) Pillbox hat
d) Newsboy cap

11. What type of lunchbox material became more common in the 1960s, replacing earlier metal designs?

a) Aluminum
b) Vinyl
c) Plastic
d) Cardboard

12. **The invention of the transistor radio in the 1960s allowed teenagers to listen to music away from home for the first time.**

a) True
b) False

13. **What school supply, first introduced in the 1960s, quickly became a staple for students?**

a) Trapper Keeper
b) Ballpoint pen
c) Felt-tip markers
d) White-out

DID YOU KNOW?

When **The Beatles** made their U.S. television debut on **The Ed Sullivan Show** in **1964**, the world changed forever. More than **73 million people** tuned in to watch the British rockers perform, officially kicking off Beatlemania and the British Invasion.

14. What was a common lunchbox theme for kids in the 1960s?

a) Batman
b) The Jetsons
c) The Monkees
d) All of the above

15. Which outdoor toy, although invented in the late 1950s, became a massive craze in the 1960s?

a) Frisbee
b) Pogo stick
c) Super Ball
d) Skip-It

16. By the early 1960s, most television sets came with remote controls.

a) True
b) False

17. Which psychedelic fabric pattern was extremely popular in 1960s fashion?

a) Plaid
b) Paisley
c) Gingham
d) Houndstooth

18. What brand of die-cast toy cars, introduced in 1968, became a sensation?

a) Tonka
b) Hot Wheels
c) Matchbox
d) Johnny Lightning

19. Which famous children's book, first published in 1963, became a classic?

a) Where the Wild Things Are
b) The Cat in the Hat
c) Green Eggs and Ham
d) Curious George

20. What fast-food chain introduced its first kids' meal in the 1960s?

a) McDonald's
b) Burger King
c) Wendy's
d) Dairy Queen

Entertainment & Culture

1. Which song by The Beatles became the first to hit #1 on the Billboard Hot 100 chart in the U.S.?

a) Love Me Do
b) I Want to Hold Your Hand
c) She Loves You
d) Please Please Me

2. What was the name of the fictional villains featured in the 1968 musical film Yellow Submarine?

a) The Rolling Tones
b) The Monkees
c) The Blue Meanies
d) The Yellow Bandits

3. The Sound of Music was the highest-grossing movie of the 1960s.

a) True
b) False

4. **Which television show, premiering in 1966, featured the first interracial kiss on American television?**

   a) I Dream of Jeannie
   b) Star Trek
   c) Mission: Impossible
   d) Bewitched

5. **What dance craze, popularized by Chubby Checker in 1960, became a nationwide sensation?**

   a) The Mashed Potato
   b) The Twist
   c) The Jerk
   d) The Watusi

6. **What novel, published in 1960, became a cultural milestone and won the Pulitzer Prize for Fiction?**

   a) Slaughterhouse-Five
   b) To Kill a Mockingbird
   c) Catch-22
   d) One Flew Over the Cuckoo's Nest

7. Which musician was famously known as the „Queen of Soul" by the end of the 1960s?

a) Diana Ross
b) Aretha Franklin
c) Etta James
d) Tina Turner

8. The Flintstones was the first animated television show to air in prime time.

a) True
b) False

9. What famous phrase did Neil Armstrong say when he stepped onto the Moon in 1969?

a) „The Eagle has landed."
b) „That's one small step for man, one giant leap for mankind."
c) „We come in peace for all mankind."
d) „Houston, we have a problem."

10. Who played James Bond in the first-ever 007 film, Dr. No (1962)?

a) Roger Moore
b) Sean Connery
c) George Lazenby
d) Timothy Dalton

11. Which fashion designer is credited with popularizing the mini skirt?

a) Coco Chanel
b) Mary Quant
c) Diane von Fürstenberg
d) Yves Saint Laurent

12. The original Batman TV series starring Adam West was a serious and dark adaptation of the comic books.

a) True
b) False

13. What hit song by The Rolling Stones features the lyrics, „Hey, hey, hey, that‘s what I say“?

a) Jumpin' Jack Flash
b) Paint It Black
c) Gimme Shelter
d) (I Can't Get No) Satisfaction

14. What groundbreaking sci-fi movie, directed by Stanley Kubrick, was released in 1968?

a) Planet of the Apes
b) 2001: A Space Odyssey
c) The Time Machine
d) The Andromeda Strain

DID YOU KNOW?

The **Space Race** reached its peak in **1969** when astronaut **Neil Armstrong** became the **first human to walk on the moon**. As he stepped onto the lunar surface, he uttered the now-famous words: "That's one small step for man, one giant leap for mankind."

15. Which popular sitcom followed the lives of a blended family with six children and their housekeeper?

a) My Three Sons
b) The Brady Bunch
c) The Partridge Family
d) Family Affair

16. What Motown group had hits like My Girl and Ain't Too Proud to Beg?

a) The Four Tops
b) The Supremes
c) The Temptations
d) The Jackson 5

17. The term „hippie“ originated in the 1960s and was first associated with the Haight-Ashbury district in San Francisco.

a) True
b) False

18. Which famous actor starred in The Great Escape and Bullitt, making him one of the biggest action stars of the decade?

a) Paul Newman
b) Clint Eastwood
c) Steve McQueen
d) Robert Redford

19. What major music festival in 1969 featured performances by Jimi Hendrix, Janis Joplin, and The Who?

a) Monterey Pop Festival
b) Isle of Wight Festival
c) Woodstock
d) Altamont Free Concert

20. Which classic variety show, premiering in 1969, introduced audiences to The Muppets?

a) The Ed Sullivan Show
b) Sesame Street
c) The Muppet Show
d) Rowan & Martin's Laugh-In

Historical Events & Headlines

1. What major event in 1963 led to the swearing-in of Lyndon B. Johnson as U.S. President?

a) Cuban Missile Crisis
b) Assassination of John F. Kennedy
c) Apollo 11 Moon landing
d) Watergate Scandal

2. Which country built the Berlin Wall in 1961?

a) Soviet Union
b) West Germany
c) East Germany
d) United States

3. The Civil Rights Act of 1964 legally ended racial segregation in the United States.

a) True
b) False

4. What famous speech did Martin Luther King Jr. deliver in 1963 during the March on Washington?

a) „We Shall Overcome“
b) „I Have a Dream“
c) „A Time for Change“
d) „The Mountaintop Speech“

5. What war dominated U.S. foreign policy in the 1960s?

a) Korean War
b) Vietnam War
c) Gulf War
d) Cold War

6. Who became the first man in space in 1961?

a) John Glenn
b) Neil Armstrong
c) Yuri Gagarin
d) Buzz Aldrin

7. Which political scandal in 1962 nearly resulted in a nuclear war between the U.S. and the Soviet Union?

a) Watergate
b) Cuban Missile Crisis
c) Iran-Contra Affair
d) Bay of Pigs Invasion

DID YOU KNOW?

Did you know that the first-ever **Happy Meal** prototype was introduced in **1968**? Though it would take another decade to become a staple at McDonald's, the fast-food giant was already testing the idea of combining **kid-friendly meals** with **small toys** to make dining out even more exciting.

8. Richard Nixon was elected president in 1960.

a) True
b) False

9. In 1967, what music festival became one of the first major rock festivals, setting the stage for Woodstock?

a) Monterey Pop Festival
b) Isle of Wight Festival
c) Altamont Speedway Free Festival
d) Newport Folk Festival

10. Which African nation gained independence from British rule in 1963?

a) Nigeria
b) Ghana
c) Kenya
d) South Africa

11. What spaceflight mission successfully landed the first humans on the Moon in 1969?

a) Apollo 10
b) Apollo 11
c) Gemini 12
d) Apollo 13

12. The U.S. successfully overthrew Fidel Castro during the Bay of Pigs invasion in 1961.

a) True
b) False

13. Who was assassinated just two months after Martin Luther King Jr. in 1968?

a) Malcolm X
b) Robert F. Kennedy
c) Medgar Evers
d) John Lennon

14. What major international sporting event was held in Mexico City in 1968?

a) FIFA World Cup
b) Summer Olympics
c) Winter Olympics
d) Commonwealth Games

15. What became a widely recognized symbol of the 1960s counterculture movement?

a) The American flag
b) The peace sign
c) The hammer and sickle
d) The yin-yang symbol

16. Who was the U.S. Chief Justice who led several landmark Supreme Court decisions expanding civil rights in the 1960s?

a) Earl Warren
b) Thurgood Marshall
c) William Rehnquist
d) Warren Burger

17. The Beatles performed their last live concert in the United States in 1966.

a) True
b) False

18. What was the name of the feminist book published by Betty Friedan in 1963 that helped ignite the women's liberation movement?

a) The Second Sex
b) The Feminine Mystique
c) A Room of One's Own
d) Women and Power

19. What was the name of the operation in which U.S. forces carried out massive aerial bombings over North Vietnam?

a) Operation Rolling Thunder
b) Operation Desert Storm
c) Operation Overlord
d) Operation Barbarossa

20. Which country withdrew from the British Commonwealth and declared itself a republic in 1961?

a) Canada
b) South Africa
c) Australia
d) India

Technology & Innovation

1. What major advancement in surgery during the 1960s allowed doctors to replace damaged joints?

a) Artificial hip replacement
b) Heart stent
c) Laser eye surgery
d) Laparoscopic surgery

2. Which major transportation innovation, introduced in 1964, changed high-speed travel in Japan?

a) Bullet train (Shinkansen)
b) Magnetic levitation train
c) Monorail system
d) High-speed subway

3. The first successful human heart transplant was performed in the 1960s.

a) True
b) False

4. What famous computer programming language, developed in the 1960s, became widely used in business and government?

a) Python
b) Java
c) COBOL
d) C++

5. Which space mission first sent humans to orbit the Moon in 1968?

a) Apollo 10
b) Apollo 8
c) Gemini 12
d) Apollo 7

6. What electronic device, introduced in 1967, revolutionized how people listened to music?

a) Cassette tape
b) Compact disc
c) 8-track tape
d) MP3 player

7. **The first ATM (Automated Teller Machine) was installed in the United States in the 1960s.**

a) True
b) False

8. **What was the name of the first successful communications satellite, launched in 1962?**

a) Sputnik 2
b) Telstar
c) Voyager 1
d) Explorer 6

9. **Which type of aircraft, introduced in the 1960s, allowed for supersonic commercial travel?**

a) Boeing 747
b) Concorde
c) Lockheed SR-71 Blackbird
d) Airbus A300

10. **Which computer scientist led the development of the first practical computer mouse in the 1960s?**

a) Alan Turing
b) Douglas Engelbart
c) Steve Jobs
d) Bill Gates

11. What significant medical imaging technique was developed in the 1960s, paving the way for modern scans?

a) X-ray imaging
b) CT scanning
c) MRI scanning
d) Ultrasound

12. The Boeing 747, the first wide-body commercial jet, was introduced in the 1960s.

a) True
b) False

13. What famous robotic device used for space exploration was first tested in the 1960s?

a) Mars Rover
b) Lunar Rover
c) Deep-sea submersible
d) Voyager probe

14. The invention of what household appliance in the 1960s made cleaning easier for homeowners?

a) Self-cleaning oven
b) Cordless vacuum
c) Dishwasher with a drying feature
d) Electric can opener

Did You Know?

In the early 1960s, **color television** took over! While black-and-white TVs had been the standard for years, networks slowly started broadcasting **shows in full color**, bringing vivid images of sports, entertainment, and news into living rooms across America. By the mid-'60s, most major TV shows, including Bonanza and Bewitched, had made the switch.

15. Which groundbreaking 1960s invention revolutionized electronic circuits by replacing bulky vacuum tubes with a smaller, more efficient alternative?

a) Microchip
b) Laser
c) Floppy disk
d) Cathode-ray tube

16. The first video game console was invented in the 1960s.

a) True
b) False

17. What breakthrough weather technology was first launched into space in the 1960s to track storms?

a) Doppler radar
b) Weather satellite
c) Thermal imaging
d) GPS

18. What major discovery in physics, confirmed in the 1960s, helped support the Big Bang theory?

a) Higgs boson
b) Cosmic microwave background radiation
c) Quantum entanglement
d) Superstring theory

19. Which automobile safety feature, made mandatory in many vehicles during the 1960s, significantly reduced fatalities?

a) Airbags
b) Seat belts
c) Anti-lock brakes
d) Crumple zones

20. What major space telescope was first conceptualized in the 1960s, eventually launching in 1990?

a) Kepler Space Telescope
b) Hubble Space Telescope
c) James Webb Space Telescope
d) Spitzer Space Telescope

Sports & Big Achievements

1. Who won the most Grand Slam singles titles in men's tennis during the 1960s?

a) Rod Laver
b) Roy Emerson
c) Ken Rosewall
d) Arthur Ashe

2. Which country won the FIFA World Cup in 1966?

a) Brazil
b) West Germany
c) England
d) Italy

3. Muhammad Ali won his first heavyweight title in 1969.

a) True
b) False

4. **What was the first Super Bowl, held in 1967, originally called?**

a) NFL-AFL Championship Game
b) Pro Football Championship
c) National Football Championship
d) Super Bowl I

5. **In 1962, Wilt Chamberlain set an NBA record by scoring how many points in a single game?**

a) 81
b) 100
c) 92
d) 89

6. **Who won the most Formula 1 World Championships during the 1960s?**

a) Jim Clark
b) Jack Brabham
c) Graham Hill
d) Jackie Stewart

7. The Summer Olympics were held in Mexico City in 1964.

a) True
b) False

8. Who became the first African American golfer to play in The Masters Tournament in 1961?

a) Charlie Sifford
b) Lee Elder
c) Calvin Peete
d) Jim Thorpe

9. What team won the most World Series championships during the 1960s?

a) Los Angeles Dodgers
b) St. Louis Cardinals
c) New York Yankees
d) San Francisco Giants

10. Which Olympic athlete set a world record by winning four gold medals in the 1960 Rome Olympics?

a) Bob Hayes
b) Wilma Rudolph
c) Cassius Clay
d) Rafer Johnson

DID YOU KNOW?

Nothing says 1960s décor like a **lava lamp**! The groovy lava lamp was invented in **1963** and quickly became a **must-have item** for every teen's bedroom or dorm room. Paired with **psychedelic posters**, **beaded curtains**, and **shag rugs**, it helped define the decade's signature funky style.

11. The Green Bay Packers won the first two Super Bowls in 1967 and 1968.

a) True
b) False

12. Which boxer famously said, „I am the greatest," and changed his name from Cassius Clay?

a) Sonny Liston
b) Joe Frazier
c) Muhammad Ali
d) George Foreman

13. Which famous racehorse won the 1964 Kentucky Derby and Belmont Stakes?

a) Northern Dancer
b) Kelso
c) Damascus
d) Majestic Prince

14. Who won the most PGA Tour events in the 1960s?

a) Jack Nicklaus
b) Arnold Palmer
c) Gary Player
d) Billy Casper

15. The 1968 Summer Olympics in Mexico City saw the first use of an all-weather synthetic track.

a) True
b) False

16. What was the first Major League Baseball team to relocate in the 1960s?

a) Washington Senators
b) Milwaukee Braves
c) Brooklyn Dodgers
d) Kansas City Athletics

17. Which college football team won three national championships during the 1960s?

a) Alabama
b) Notre Dame
c) Texas
d) USC

18. Which sport made its debut at the 1964 Summer Olympics in Tokyo?

a) Judo
b) Volleyball
c) Badminton
d) Handball

19. Who was the first NBA player to surpass 25,000 career points in the 1960s?

a) Bill Russell
b) Wilt Chamberlain
c) Jerry West
d) Elgin Baylor

20. What was significant about Bob Beamon's long jump at the 1968 Olympics?

a) It was the first jump over 30 feet
b) It set a world record that lasted for 23 years
c) It was disqualified for wind assistance
d) He broke both ankles on landing

REMEMBERING THE PSYCHEDELIC '60s!

The 1960s were a decade of **change**, **rebellion**, and **unforgettable moments**. It was the time of **Beatlemania**, the **space race**, and **civil rights marches**. **Music** got louder, **fashion** got bolder, and people everywhere were **pushing the boundaries** of what was possible. By the end of the '60s, humans had even walked on the **moon**!

Whether you were grooving to The Beatles, watching Neil Armstrong's historic step, or protesting for change, the '60s were truly a time like no other!

Talk & Think About the 1960s

Use these fun questions to relive old memories, share your favorite stories, or spark up a conversation with loved ones!

1. What was the most exciting thing you remember about the '60s? A concert, a major event, or a personal milestone?

2. What music defined your teenage years? Were you twisting to Chubby Checker or swaying to Simon & Garfunkel?

3. Think back to your favorite outfit—bell-bottoms, tie-dye, or maybe a mod mini skirt?

4. What TV shows kept you glued to the screen? Star Trek, The Andy Griffith Show, or Laugh-In?

5. What was your favorite hangout spot—drive-ins, diners, or the local record store?

6. If you could relive one day from the '60s, which would it be and why?

7. Do you remember your first big purchase? Maybe a transistor radio, a brand-new record player, or your very first car?

8. What games or activities did you enjoy most with friends?

9. How did your family spend weekends? Road trips, concerts, or backyard barbecues?

Write About the 1960s

Jot down your favorite memories from this groovy decade! Maybe it was your first love, a historic event you witnessed, or the thrill of a new experience.

The '60s were a whirlwind of change, music, and unforgettable moments—let's keep those stories alive!

CHAPTER THREE

The 1970s

Ah, the 1970s—where **bell-bottoms** were big, **sideburns** were bigger, and **disco** reigned supreme! This was the decade of Stayin' Alive with the **Bee Gees**, blasting American Pie by **Don McLean** on the radio and slow dancing to Let's Get It On by **Marvin Gaye**. Whether you were rocking out to **Led Zeppelin**, singing along to **Carole King's** It's Too Late, or getting down to Superstition by **Stevie Wonder**, music was the heartbeat of the '70s.

But the '70s weren't just about the tunes. It was a **wild**, **colorful**, and **game-changing** time. The world tuned in as **NASA's Apollo program** sent its final missions to the moon. **Muhammad Ali** stunned the world with **The Rumble in the Jungle**, and **Billie Jean King** took on **Bobby Riggs** in the famous "**Battle of the Sexes**." Families gathered around their **wood-paneled TVs** to catch the latest episodes of **Happy Days**, **Charlie's Angels**, and **The Brady Bunch**. And who could forget the excitement of seeing **Star Wars** hit the big screen in

1977, forever changing the galaxy of pop culture?

It was also the era of **pet rocks**, **mood rings**, and the rise of the **8-track tape**—perfect for blasting Bohemian Rhapsody by **Queen** during a Saturday night cruise. **Roller rinks** were packed with **skaters** grooving to Le Freak by Chic, and **arcades** were buzzing with kids playing **Pong** for hours on end. And if you weren't at the rink or arcade, you might have been on the couch watching **Saturday Night Live** make its legendary debut.

Whether you spent your time in **platform shoes**, a **denim jacket**, or a **tie-dye shirt**, one thing's for sure, the '70s were a time of unforgettable moments.

So dust off that lava lamp, put a record on the turntable, and get ready to take a far-out trip down memory lane. The '70s were bold, loud, and unforgettable—just like the memories you're about to relive!

Daily Life & Childhood Memories

1. What popular toy of the 1970s featured small, colorful people that fit into different vehicles and playsets?

a) Fisher-Price Little People
b) Playmobil
c) LEGO Minifigures
d) Polly Pocket

2. What fabric was commonly used in bell-bottom pants and leisure suits during the '70s?

a) Polyester
b) Velvet
c) Corduroy
d) Denim

3. The Rubik's Cube was invented in the 1970s.

a) True
b) False

4. What popular school supply became a fashion statement and was often traded among kids?

a) Trapper Keeper
b) Scratch 'n Sniff Stickers
c) Lisa Frank Notebooks
d) Gel Pens

5. Which snack, introduced in the '70s, became a favorite lunchbox treat?

a) Twinkies
b) Pop-Tarts
c) Hostess Ding Dongs
d) Fruit Roll-Ups

6. What was a common way for kids to listen to music on the go in the 1970s?

a) Walkman
b) 8-Track Player
c) Portable CD Player
d) MP3 Player

DID YOU KNOW?

Before the Sony Walkman hit the scene, music lovers in the 1970s relied on **8-track tapes** to take their favorite tunes on the go. These chunky cartridges were a staple in cars and home stereo systems, though they were eventually replaced by **cassettes** in the **late '70s**.

7. The TV dinner became widely popular in the 1970s due to busy family lifestyles.

a) True
b) False

8. What popular board game, first released in 1974, involved buying properties and making deals?

a) Monopoly
b) The Game of Life
c) Pay Day
d) Connect Four

9. Which 1970s TV show featured a blended family of six kids and a wise housekeeper?

a) The Brady Bunch
b) Happy Days
c) Good Times
d) Three's Company

10. What shoe style featuring thick soles was a huge trend in the '70s?

a) Platform shoes
b) Converse All-Stars
c) Loafers
d) Sandals

11. The first video game home console to be sold to the public, the Atari 2600, was released in the 1970s.

a) True
b) False

12. What common school punishment involved writing the same phrase repeatedly on a chalkboard?

a) Writing sentences
b) Detention
c) Getting sent to the principal's office
d) Cleaning erasers

13. What household item, often found in the '70s, featured rotating colored lights and created a psychedelic effect?

a) Lava lamp
b) Disco ball
c) Blacklight poster
d) Strobe light

14. What '70s novelty toy involved little "pets" that came in a small plastic box?

a) Pet Rock
b) Tamagotchi
c) Cabbage Patch Kids
d) Furby

15. "Schoolhouse Rock!" was a popular educational TV program in the 1970s.

a) True
b) False

16. What was a popular hairstyle for men in the 1970s?

a) Pompadour
b) Mullet
c) Feathered hair
d) Mohawk

17. What toy allowed kids to create "art" by spinning paper while dripping paint?

a) Spirograph
b) Lite-Brite
c) Etch A Sketch
d) Spin Art

18. Which school lunch item first hit the shelves in 1971?

a) Lunchables
b) Capri Sun
c) Cup Noodles
d) Go-Gurt

19. Skateboarding saw a huge rise in popularity during the 1970s.

a) True
b) False

20. What color-changing toy became a craze in the 1970s?

a) Glow Worm
b) Chia Pet
c) Mood Ring
d) Lite-Brite

Entertainment & Culture

1. What 1970s TV show featured a group of high school friends hanging out at Arnold's Drive-In?

a) Welcome Back, Kotter
b) Happy Days
c) The Wonder Years
d) Laverne & Shirley

2. What famous phrase came from the 1976 movie Taxi Driver starring Robert De Niro?

a) „You talkin' to me?"
b) „I'll be back."
c) „Say hello to my little friend!"
d) „We're gonna need a bigger boat."

3. The first Rocky movie was released in the 1970s.

a) True
b) False

4. What singer became known as the „Queen of Disco“ in the late 1970s?

a) Diana Ross
b) Donna Summer
c) Gloria Gaynor
d) Cher

5. Which 1970s movie was the highest-grossing film of the decade?

a) Jaws
b) Star Wars
c) Rocky
d) The Godfather

6. Who hosted The Tonight Show for the majority of the 1970s?

a) David Letterman
b) Jay Leno
c) Johnny Carson
d) Dick Cavett

7. The phrase „May the Force be with you“ became famous in the 1970s.

a) True
b) False

DID YOU KNOW?

When **Saturday Night Fever** hit theaters in **1977, disco fever took over the world**. The film, starring John Travolta, helped turn the **Bee Gees' soundtrack** into one of the **best-selling albums** of all time, and soon, everyone was hitting the dance floor in bell-bottoms and platform shoes.

8. What band released the hit song Hotel California in 1976?

a) Fleetwood Mac
b) The Eagles
c) Led Zeppelin
d) The Rolling Stones

9. Which actress played Princess Leia in Star Wars?

a) Meryl Streep
b) Sigourney Weaver
c) Carrie Fisher
d) Goldie Hawn

10. What fashion trend became a symbol of the disco era?

a) Shoulder pads
b) Platform shoes
c) Grunge flannel
d) Cargo pants

11. The Brady Bunch debuted in the 1970s.

a) True
b) False

12. What popular books, which later became a hit movie franchise, debuted in 1974 with Carrie?

a) The Twilight Saga
b) The Harry Potter Series
c) Stephen King's horror novels
d) The Lord of the Rings

13. What type of dance became a sensation with the rise of disco?

a) The Charleston
b) The Hustle
c) The Macarena
d) The Robot

14. Who played Danny Zuko in the 1978 movie Grease?

a) Harrison Ford
b) John Travolta
c) Richard Gere
d) Sylvester Stallone

15. The Sony Walkman was introduced in the 1970s.

a) True
b) False

16. What Saturday morning cartoon featured a mystery-solving gang and their talking Great Dane?

a) The Jetsons
b) The Flintstones
c) Scooby-Doo, Where Are You!
d) Super Friends

17. Who became a pop culture icon after starring in Saturday Night Fever?

a) John Travolta
b) Patrick Swayze
c) Tom Cruise
d) Al Pacino

18. Which sitcom featured a family living in an apartment in Chicago and coined the phrase „Dy-no-mite!"?

a) Good Times
b) All in the Family
c) Sanford and Son
d) Diff'rent Strokes

19. David Bowie's alter ego, Ziggy Stardust, debuted in the 1970s.

a) True
b) False

20. What 1970s TV show, set during the Korean War, became one of the most beloved and highest-rated series of all time?

a) All in the Family
b) The Mary Tyler Moore Show
c) Happy Days
d) M*A*S*H

Historical Events & Headlines

1. Who became the U.S. president after Richard Nixon resigned in 1974?

a) Jimmy Carter
b) Gerald Ford
c) Ronald Reagan
d) Lyndon B. Johnson

2. What major international conflict ended in 1975?

a) Korean War
b) Vietnam War
c) Gulf War
d) Six-Day War

3. The Watergate scandal led to the impeachment of Richard Nixon.

a) True
b) False

4. Which country did the U.S. establish diplomatic relations with for the first time in 1979?

a) China
b) Cuba
c) North Korea
d) Iran

5. What U.S. state legalized abortion first, in 1970, before Roe v. Wade?

a) New York
b) Texas
c) California
d) Florida

6. Who was the leader of the Soviet Union for most of the 1970s?

a) Mikhail Gorbachev
b) Nikita Khrushchev
c) Leonid Brezhnev
d) Boris Yeltsin

7. The U.S. celebrated its bicentennial in 1976.

a) True
b) False

8. Which African country gained independence from Portugal in 1975?

a) Angola
b) Kenya
c) South Africa
d) Zimbabwe

9. What was the name of the peace agreement signed between Israel and Egypt in 1978?

a) Oslo Accords
b) Camp David Accords
c) Geneva Agreement
d) Cairo Peace Treaty

10. The Iranian Revolution of 1979 led to the overthrow of which leader?

a) Saddam Hussein
b) The Shah of Iran
c) Gamal Abdel Nasser
d) Ayatollah Khomeini

11. **The first Earth Day was celebrated in 1970.**

a) True
b) False

12. **What was the name of the nuclear power plant that had a major accident in 1979?**

a) Chernobyl
b) Three Mile Island
c) Fukushima
d) Hanford

13. **Which organization was founded in 1971 to focus on environmental issues?**

a) Sierra Club
b) World Wildlife Fund
c) Greenpeace
d) Environmental Protection Agency

14. Who was the first U.S. president to visit China while in office?

a) John F. Kennedy
b) Richard Nixon
c) Gerald Ford
d) Jimmy Carter

15. The Equal Rights Amendment (ERA) was ratified in the 1970s.

a) True
b) False

16. In 1972, what sporting event was tragically affected by a terrorist attack?

a) Winter Olympics in Sapporo
b) Summer Olympics in Munich
c) FIFA World Cup
d) Super Bowl VI

17. What major discovery did NASA's Viking 1 spacecraft make in 1976?

a) First close-up images of Saturn
b) Evidence of liquid water on Mars
c) First successful Mars landing
d) Discovery of an exoplanet

18. Who was the U.K. Prime Minister for most of the 1970s?

a) Margaret Thatcher
b) Harold Wilson
c) Edward Heath
d) James Callaghan

19. The Concorde supersonic passenger jet entered commercial service in the 1970s.

a) True
b) False

20. What political scandal in the U.S. led to widespread mistrust in government during the 1970s?

a) The Pentagon Papers
b) Iran-Contra Affair
c) Watergate
d) Teapot Dome Scandal

DID YOU KNOW?

In **1972**, **Pong** became the **first commercially successful video game**, marking the beginning of the home gaming industry. The simple tennis-like game created by Atari may seem basic by today's standards. Still, at the time, it was revolutionary!

Technology & Innovation

1. What company introduced the first personal computer, the Altair 8800, in 1975?

a) IBM
b) Microsoft
c) MITS
d) Apple

2. Which medical imaging technology was first used in the 1970s?

a) X-ray
b) CT scan
c) Ultrasound
d) MRI

3. The first email was sent in the 1970s.

a) True
b) False

4. What invention, first widely introduced in the 1970s, revolutionized the way people stored and listened to music?

a) Cassette tape
b) Compact disc (CD)
c) MP3 player
d) 8-track tape

5. Which company released the first commercially available video game console, the Magnavox Odyssey, in 1972?

a) Atari
b) Nintendo
c) Magnavox
d) Sega

6. The first space station, launched in 1971, was called what?

a) Skylab
b) Mir
c) Salyut 1
d) ISS

7. The first mobile phone call was made in the 1970s.

a) True
b) False

8. What was the name of the first Mars probe to successfully land on the planet in 1976?

a) Mariner 9
b) Viking 1
c) Pioneer 10
d) Voyager 1

9. What new type of display technology was introduced in calculators and digital watches in the 1970s?

a) LCD
b) Plasma
c) LED
d) OLED

10. Which tech company was founded in 1976 in a garage?

a) Microsoft
b) Apple
c) Intel
d) IBM

11. The first barcode scanner was used in the 1970s.

a) True
b) False

12. What home entertainment breakthrough allowed consumers to record and watch television shows at home?

a) DVD
b) VHS
c) Betamax
d) LaserDisc

13. What energy crisis in the 1970s led to significant advances in fuel efficiency and alternative energy research?

a) The OPEC Oil Embargo
b) The Great Depression
c) The Cold War
d) The Dot-Com Crash

14. Which handheld electronic game system, introduced in 1979, paved the way for future gaming devices?

a) Game Boy
b) Atari Lynx
c) Microvision
d) Nintendo Game & Watch

DID YOU KNOW?

One of the strangest fads of the 1970s was the **Pet Rock**. Launched in **1975**, this „low-maintenance pet" was literally just a **smooth rock in a box** with breathing holes—yet millions of people bought one!

15. The first artificial heart was implanted in a human in the 1970s.

a) True
b) False

16. What NASA project in the 1970s focused on reusable spacecraft?

a) Apollo
b) Space Shuttle
c) Gemini
d) Mercury

17. Which company released the world's first pocket calculator in 1972?

a) Casio
b) Texas Instruments
c) Hewlett-Packard
d) Sharp

18. GPS technology was first developed for civilian use in the 1970s.

a) True
b) False

19. What breakthrough fuel-saving car was introduced in the U.S. during the 1970s oil crisis?

a) Toyota Prius
b) Honda Civic
c) Ford Mustang
d) Chevrolet Corvette

20. What invention, developed in the 1970s, transformed how people stored and transferred digital data?

a) USB Flash Drive
b) Compact Disc (CD)
c) Floppy Disk
d) Hard Drive

Sports & Big Achievements

1. Who won the FIFA World Cup in 1970, showcasing one of the greatest teams in soccer history?

a) Argentina
b) West Germany
c) Brazil
d) Italy

2. In 1973, which horse won the Triple Crown, setting records that still stand today?

a) Secretariat
b) Seattle Slew
c) Affirmed
d) Spectacular Bid

3. Which team won three consecutive Super Bowls in the 1970s?

a) Miami Dolphins
b) Pittsburgh Steelers
c) Dallas Cowboys
d) None—no team won three in a row

4. Nadia Comaneci became the first gymnast to score a perfect 10 at the 1976 Montreal Olympics.

a) True
b) False

5. The „Battle of the Sexes" tennis match in 1973 featured Billie Jean King playing against which male tennis player?

a) Jimmy Connors
b) Björn Borg
c) John McEnroe
d) Bobby Riggs

6. Who was the first African American to win a men's singles title at Wimbledon, achieving this milestone in 1975?

a) Arthur Ashe
b) Althea Gibson
c) Rod Laver
d) John Newcombe

7. The 1972 Summer Olympics in Munich were the first Olympic Games to feature women's basketball.

a) True
b) False

8. Which team ended the 1972 NFL season undefeated, making them the only team in history to achieve a perfect season?

a) Dallas Cowboys
b) Pittsburgh Steelers
c) Miami Dolphins
d) Oakland Raiders

9. Who became the first player in NBA history to average a triple-double for an entire season, accomplishing the feat in the early 1970s?

a) Oscar Robertson
b) Kareem Abdul-Jabbar
c) Magic Johnson
d) Larry Bird

10. Muhammad Ali lost to George Foreman in the famous „Rumble in the Jungle“ fight in 1974.

a) True
b) False

11. What historic event happened during the 1972 Olympic men's basketball final?

a) The game was delayed due to a power outage

b) The Soviet Union controversially defeated the U.S. in the final seconds

c) The U.S. won its eighth consecutive gold medal

d) The final was postponed due to a protest

12. Which Major League Baseball team won back-to-back-to-back World Series titles from 1972 to 1974?

a) New York Yankees

b) Oakland Athletics

c) Cincinnati Reds

d) Baltimore Orioles

DID YOU KNOW?

By the **late '70s, microwave ovens** were becoming a kitchen essential. They allowed people to cook meals in minutes instead of hours, completely changing the way families prepared dinner. Suddenly, **TV dinners and instant popcorn** were all the rage.

13. In 1977, which team won its first NBA championship, led by Bill Walton?

a) Philadelphia 76ers
b) Los Angeles Lakers
c) Portland Trail Blazers
d) Boston Celtics

14. True or False: Jack Nicklaus won all four major golf championships in a single calendar year during the 1970s.

a) True
b) False

15. Which city hosted the 1976 Summer Olympics?

a) Montreal
b) Los Angeles
c) Mexico City
d) Munich

16. Who was the leading scorer of the 1970s in the NBA, finishing the decade with the most total points?

a) Wilt Chamberlain
b) Julius Erving
c) Kareem Abdul-Jabbar
d) George Gervin

17. Which athlete won seven gold medals in swimming at the 1972 Olympics, setting multiple world records?

a) Janet Evans
b) Debbie Meyer
c) Shirley Babashoff
d) Mark Spitz

18. During the 1970s, the Indianapolis 500 was won by a female driver.

a) True
b) False

19. Which hockey team won four consecutive Stanley Cups from 1976 to 1979?

a) Montreal Canadiens
b) Boston Bruins
c) New York Islanders
d) Philadelphia Flyers

20. Who was named Sports Illustrated's Sportsman of the Year in 1978 after an incredible baseball season?

a) Pete Rose
b) Reggie Jackson
c) Carl Yastrzemski
d) Steve Carlton

REMEMBERING THE SENSATIONAL '70s!

The 1970s were a time of **bold fashion**, **unforgettable music**, **groundbreaking technology**, and moments that changed history. It was the decade of **disco** and **rock 'n' roll**, **lava lamps** and **shag carpets**, **bell-bottoms** and **platform shoes**. Families gathered around the TV to watch **Happy Days** and **M*A*S*H**. At the same time, kids spent their afternoons on **banana seat bikes** or playing with **Stretch Armstrong**.

Did you know that in **1977**, the world was introduced to **Star Wars**, changing movies forever? Or that the **first-ever email** was sent in **1971**, paving the way for how we communicate today? The '70s gave us the **Walkman**, **mood rings**, **digital watches**, and the birth of **video games**—imagine life without **Pong**!

The world was changing, too. The decade saw the **first Earth Day** in **1970**, the **rise of women's rights** and **environmental activism**, and the **end of the Vietnam War**. Meanwhile, sports fans were treated to epic moments, from **Muhammad Ali's** biggest fights to the **Pittsburgh Steelers** dominating the NFL.

Whether you were tuning in to American Bandstand, cruising in a Mustang, or roller-skating at the local rink, the '70s were full of unforgettable moments.

Talk & Think About the 1970s

Use these fun questions to spark memories, share stories, and bring the '70s back to life!

1. What's one of your favorite memories from the '70s? Was it playing outside until the streetlights came on, spending weekends at the roller rink, or rocking out to your favorite band?

2. What was your go-to fashion statement? Did you own a pair of platform shoes, wear bell-bottoms with pride, or layer on beads and fringe?

3. What was your favorite song to blast on the radio? Did you groove to disco, rock out to Led Zeppelin, or sing along to The Carpenters?

4. Do you remember your first time seeing Star Wars or another big '70s movie? What was it like to experience the blockbuster era for the first time?

5. What TV show could you not miss? Were you hooked on The Brady Bunch, laughing at The Jeffersons, or solving mysteries with Columbo?
6. How did you spend your weekends? Was it drive-in movies, hanging out at the arcade, or piling into the car for a long road trip?
7. What was your first job? Did you work at a diner, a movie theater, or a local shop? And how much did you make back then?
8. Did you follow the big events of the decade? What do you remember about the Watergate scandal, the energy crisis, or the end of the Vietnam War?
9. Do you remember the excitement of new technology? Did you ever use an 8-track player, see a microwave for the first time, or play Pong on a home console?
10. What was your first car like? Was it a muscle car, a station wagon, or a reliable little beater that got you where you needed to go?

Write About the 1970s

Take a moment to jot down your favorite '70s memories. Maybe it was your first big concert, a summer filled with adventure, or the thrill of watching your favorite team win a championship.

The '70s were full of change, excitement, and unforgettable trends. Whether you were rocking out at a concert, saving up for the latest gadget, or watching history unfold on the evening news, your stories are a part of what made this decade so special. Let's keep the memories alive!!

CHAPTER FOUR

The 1980s

Big hair, **neon colors**, **arcade games**, and **boom boxes**! Welcome to one of the most unforgettable decades of all time! The 1980s were **bold**, **loud**, and **packed with pop culture moments** that still make us smile. If you ever rocked a pair of **leg warmers**, spent hours perfecting your **Pac-Man** skills, or recorded your favorite songs off the radio onto a **cassette tape**, you know exactly what made this decade so special.

Music was everywhere, blasting from **Walkmans** and **car stereos** with hits like **Michael Jackson's** "Billie Jean," **Madonna's** "Like a Virgin," and **Bon Jovi's** "Livin' on a Prayer." Whether you were slow-dancing to "Every Breath You Take" by **The Police** or getting pumped up with **Queen's** "Another One Bites the Dust," the '80s had a song for every mood. And let's not forget **MTV**! Launched in 1981, it changed music forever, giving us epic videos like **A-ha's** "Take on Me" and **Prince's** "When Doves Cry."

But the '80s weren't just about music. This was the decade of **E.T.** phoning home, the **Breakfast Club** skipping detention, and **Indiana Jones** cracking his whip. If you weren't at the movie theater watching **Top Gun** or **Back to the Future**, you were probably at home trying to solve a **Rubik's Cube** or watching **sitcoms** like **Family Ties** and **The Golden Girls**.

Go grab a can of New Coke, pop in a mixtape, and get ready to relive the magic of the 1980s, a decade that was totally rad!

Daily Life & Childhood Memories

1. **What was the name of the popular doll line from the 1980s that came with a unique birth certificate and was known for its adoption theme?**

   a) My Child Dolls
   b) Cabbage Patch Kids
   c) Pound Puppies
   d) Strawberry Shortcake

2. **Which of these fashion trends was NOT popular in the 1980s?**

   a) Leg warmers
   b) Shoulder pads
   c) Flannel shirts
   d) Jelly shoes

3. **In the 1980s, Trapper Keepers were banned in some schools because teachers thought they were too distracting.**

   a) True
   b) False

4. What was the name of the scratch-and-sniff stickers that kids collected in the 1980s, often featuring fun designs and scents like bubblegum and pizza?

a) Smelly Stickers
b) Scratchies
c) Stinky Stickers
d) Sniff 'n' Stick

5. What was the most common way kids recorded their favorite songs in the 1980s?

a) CDs
b) Cassette tapes
c) Vinyl records
d) MP3 player

6. The most popular home computer of the 1980s, selling millions of units and introducing kids to gaming and programming, was the:

a) Apple Macintosh
b) IBM PC
c) Commodore 64
d) Atari 5200

7. McDonald's Happy Meals first became available in the 1980s.

a) True
b) False

DID YOU KNOW?

On **August 1, 1981, MTV launched** and changed the music industry forever. The very **first music video** played was **Video Killed the Radio Star** by **The Buggles**, setting the stage for a decade dominated by music videos and pop culture icons like Michael Jackson and Madonna.

8. What was the name of the popular schoolyard game that involved jumping over a spinning rope with a weighted ball on one end that was attached to a child's ankle?

a) Hyper Jump
b) Skip-It
c) Ankle Bouncer
d) Foot Twister

9. Which drink was discontinued in 1985 after a major public backlash, only to return later due to popular demand?

a) Tab
b) New Coke
c) Crystal Pepsi
d) Hi-C Ecto Cooler

10. Which toy brand allowed kids to create colorful pictures by placing tiny plastic pegs into a backlit board?

a) Magna Doodle
b) Lite-Brite
c) Etch A Sketch
d) Spirograph

11. In the 1980s, it was common for kids to call a 1-900 number to hear messages from their favorite TV characters or celebrities.

a) True
b) False

12. What was the name of the sticker album series that featured gross-out parody versions of Cabbage Patch Kids?

a) Garbage Pail Kids
b) Wacky Packages
c) Slime Stickers
d) Madball Mayhem

13. What was the must-have footwear of the late 1980s, known for its pump-up air feature?

a) Converse All-Stars
b) LA Gear Lights
c) Reebok Pumps
d) Vans Sk8-Hi

14. Which of these items was a staple in most 1980s school lunches?

a) Lunchables
b) Go-Gurt
c) Capri Sun
d) Sunny Delight

15. What was the name of the popular playset that let kids create gummy, plastic creatures by pouring a liquid into metal molds and heating it up?

a) Creepy Crawlers
b) Fun Factory
c) Slime Time
d) Easy-Bake Bugs

16. Sticker albums were one of the biggest collecting crazes of the 1980s, with kids trading stickers like currency.

a) True
b) False

17. What was the name of the scented dolls that smelled like different desserts and came with their own little pet?

a) Cupcake Cuties
b) Strawberry Shortcake
c) Lil' Sprouts
d) Candy Kids

18. What brand of jeans was considered the ultimate status symbol for teens in the 1980s?

a) Guess
b) Wrangler
c) JNCO
d) Calvin Klein

19. What was the name of the toy line where kids could „transform" the dolls by flipping their dresses, turning them from a cupcake into a doll?

a) Magic Blossoms
b) Cupcake Surprise
c) Flip & Fun
d) Secret Keepers

20. What was the name of the game system that launched in 1985 and helped revive the video game industry after the early '80s crash?

a) Sega Genesis
b) Atari 7800
c) Super Nintendo
d) Nintendo Entertainment System (NES)

Entertainment & Culture

1. Which 1980s movie featured the famous line "I feel the need... the need for speed"?

a) Back to the Future
b) Top Gun
c) The Terminator
d) Ghostbusters

2. Who was the first artist to have a music video played on MTV when it launched in 1981?

a) Michael Jackson
b) The Buggles
c) Madonna
d) Prince

3. In the 1980s, shoulder pads were a major fashion trend for both men and women.

a) True
b) False

4. What was the name of the robotic toy that could move and talk, becoming a huge hit with kids in the '80s?

a) Teddy Ruxpin
b) My Buddy
c) Chatty Cathy
d) Kid Sister

5. Which iconic book series, first published in the 1980s, followed a group of kids who ran their own babysitting business?

a) The Baby-Sitters Club
b) Sweet Valley High
c) Goosebumps
d) Choose Your Own Adventure

6. What 1980s sitcom featured an alien from the planet Melmac who loved eating cats?

a) Mork & Mindy
b) Alf
c) Small Wonder
d) Perfect Strangers

7. Madonna's first Billboard Hot 100 No. 1 hit was "Like a Virgin."

a) True
b) False

DID YOU KNOW?

The **Rubik's Cube**, introduced **worldwide** in **1980**, became an instant hit. Millions of people spent hours twisting and turning the colorful puzzle, trying to solve it in record time. Some never did!

8. In which movie did Molly Ringwald's character have her 16th birthday forgotten by her family?

a) Pretty in Pink
b) Sixteen Candles
c) The Breakfast Club
d) St. Elmo's Fire

9. What was the best-selling video game of the 1980s?

a) The Legend of Zelda
b) Super Mario Bros.
c) Tetris
d) Pac-Man

10. Which famous slogan was coined by Wendy's in their 1984 advertising campaign?

a) "Have it your way"
b) "Where's the beef?"
c) "I'm lovin' it"
d) "Finger-lickin' good"

11. The first Walkman, introduced by Sony in the early 1980s, only played radio stations and could not play cassette tapes.

a) True
b) False

12. Which popular talk show host debuted their show in 1986, quickly becoming one of the most influential figures in television?

a) David Letterman
b) Oprah Winfrey
c) Phil Donahue
d) Arsenio Hall

13. What song and dance craze took over the world in 1981 with a music video that featured zombies and a famous red jacket?

a) „Beat It"
b) „Thriller"
c) „Super Freak"
d) „Funky Town"

14. Which 1980s movie villain famously said, "No, I am your father"?

a) The Joker (Batman)
b) Freddy Krueger (A Nightmare on Elm Street)
c) Darth Vader (Star Wars: The Empire Strikes Back)
d) Biff Tannen (Back to the Future)

15. What type of pants became a fashion craze in the 1980s, known for being brightly colored and skin-tight at the bottom?

a) Parachute pants
b) Cargo pants
c) Hammer pants
d) JNCO jeans

16. The "Macarena" was the biggest dance craze of the 1980s.

a) True
b) False

17. Who starred as Indiana Jones in the hit adventure film series that began in the 1980s?

a) Tom Cruise
b) Harrison Ford
c) Kurt Russell
d) Mel Gibson

18. What arcade game featuring a jumping plumber became a massive hit in the early 1980s?

a) Donkey Kong
b) Centipede
c) Frogger
d) Galaga

19. Which 1980s pop star was known as the „Prince of Pop“ and had a signature white glove?

a) Michael Jackson
b) George Michael
c) Prince
d) Rick Astley

20. What 1980s TV show featured a team of Vietnam War veterans who became mercenaries and drove a black GMC van?

a) The A-Team
b) Knight Rider
c) Magnum, P.I.
d) Miami Vice

Historical Events & Headlines

1. Which U.S. president was shot in an assassination attempt in 1981 but survived?

a) Jimmy Carter
b) Ronald Reagan
c) George H.W. Bush
d) Richard Nixon

2. The Chernobyl nuclear disaster occurred in which country in 1986?

a) Russia
b) Ukraine
c) Poland
d) Belarus

3. The Berlin Wall was torn down in 1985.

a) True
b) False

4. What was the name of the first woman appointed to the U.S. Supreme Court in 1981?

a) Ruth Bader Ginsburg
b) Sandra Day O'Connor
c) Sonia Sotomayor
d) Elena Kagan

5. The Challenger space shuttle disaster, which tragically killed all seven crew members, including teacher Christa McAuliffe, occurred in which year?

a) 1984
b) 1985
c) 1986
d) 1987

6. Which war began in 1980 and lasted for nearly a decade, leading to devastating losses for both sides?

a) Falklands War
b) Iran-Iraq War
c) Soviet-Afghan War
d) Lebanon Civil War

7. In 1989, protests in Tiananmen Square ended peacefully with no military intervention.

a) True
b) False

DID YOU KNOW?

In **1982, Billy Joel's 52nd Street** became the **first album ever released on compact disc (CD)**. The CD quickly became the preferred music format, eventually replacing vinyl records and cassettes.

8. What major global event took place in Los Angeles in 1984, bringing international athletes together despite a Soviet-led boycott?

a) World Expo
b) FIFA World Cup
c) Olympic Games
d) United Nations Summit

9. Who became the first elected female prime minister of a major European country, serving throughout the 1980s?

a) Indira Gandhi
b) Margaret Thatcher
c) Angela Merkel
d) Benazir Bhutto

10. The stock market crash of October 19, 1987, which saw the largest single-day percentage decline in the Dow Jones Industrial Average, was called:

a) Black Monday
b) The Great Recession
c) The Market Meltdown
d) The Wall Street Collapse

11. The personal computer became widely available to the public for the first time in the 1980s.

a) True
b) False

12. Which Cold War-era U.S. president made the famous demand, "Mr. Gorbachev, tear down this wall!" in 1987?

a) Richard Nixon
b) Jimmy Carter
c) Ronald Reagan
d) George H.W. Bush

13. What was the name of the high-profile environmental disaster that occurred in Alaska in 1989, spilling millions of gallons of crude oil into the ocean?

a) Three Mile Island Spill
b) Exxon Valdez Oil Spill
c) Deepwater Horizon Disaster
d) BP Gulf Oil Spill

14. In 1982, which British territory was invaded by Argentina, leading to a brief but intense war?

a) Gibraltar
b) Falkland Islands
c) Bermuda
d) Saint Helena

15. What was the name of the anti-apartheid leader who remained imprisoned for most of the 1980s before being released in 1990?

a) Desmond Tutu
b) Nelson Mandela
c) Steve Biko
d) Kofi Annan

16. MTV launched in 1983 as the first-ever 24-hour cable news channel.

a) True
b) False

17. What was the first country to introduce the concept of the "Internet" with the development of ARPANET, a precursor to the modern web?

a) United States
b) United Kingdom
c) Germany
d) Japan

18. Which revolutionary movement led to the ousting of Philippine President Ferdinand Marcos in 1986?

a) The Velvet Revolution
b) The People Power Revolution
c) The Jasmine Revolution
d) The Orange Revolution

19. Which landmark event in 1985 led to an agreement between the United States and the Soviet Union to begin arms reduction talks?

a) Reykjavík Summit
b) Camp David Accords
c) INF Treaty Signing
d) Geneva Summit

20. The 1980s saw the rise of a new health crisis that would change global medicine and public awareness forever. What was this crisis?

a) Mad Cow Disease
b) SARS Epidemic
c) HIV/AIDS Epidemic
d) The Avian Flu

Technology & Innovation

1. **What was the name of the first mass-market personal computer released by IBM in 1981?**

   a) Apple Macintosh
   b) IBM PC
   c) Commodore 64
   d) TRS-80

2. **The CD (compact disc) was introduced in the 1980s as a revolutionary new way to listen to music. What year was the first commercial CD player released?**

   a) 1980
   b) 1982
   c) 1985
   d) 1987

3. **The first version of Microsoft Windows was released in 1989.**

   a) True
   b) False

4. What was the name of the portable mobile phone released in 1983 that weighed over two pounds and cost nearly $4,000?

a) Nokia 5110
b) Motorola DynaTAC 8000X
c) Sony WalkiePhone
d) Ericsson M900

5. What was the name of the first commercially available disposable camera, introduced in the 1980s, making photography more accessible and convenient?

a) Kodak FunSaver
b) Fujifilm QuickSnap
c) Polaroid OneStep
d) Canon Snappy

6. What technological breakthrough, first used in the 1980s, allowed cars to monitor engine performance and reduce emissions?

a) Turbocharging
b) Electronic fuel injection
c) Anti-lock brakes
d) Catalytic converters

7. The first-ever laptop computer was introduced in 1985 by Apple.

a) True
b) False

8. The Hubble Space Telescope, one of the most famous telescopes in history, was originally supposed to launch in 1986. Why was its launch delayed?

a) A problem with its lens
b) Budget cuts
c) The Challenger disaster
d) Software issues

9. Which company released the first-ever consumer camcorder in 1983, making home video recording more accessible?

a) Panasonic
b) Sony
c) JVC
d) Canon

10. What iconic gaming character, introduced in 1981, started out as „Jumpman" before becoming one of the most famous video game mascots ever?

a) Sonic the Hedgehog
b) Pac-Man
c) Mario
d) Donkey Kong

11. The first space shuttle to be launched into orbit was Columbia in 1981.

a) True
b) False

12. What was the name of the first major home computer released by Apple in 1984, famous for its graphical user interface and iconic Super Bowl commercial?

a) Apple IIe
b) Macintosh
c) Lisa
d) PowerBook

13. What scientific discovery, announced in 1985, led to worldwide environmental action and the banning of certain chemicals?

a) The depletion of the ozone layer
b) The discovery of dark matter
c) The human genome mapping project
d) The first exoplanet discovery

DID YOU KNOW?

During the **holiday season** of 1983, **Cabbage Patch Kids** caused nationwide shopping chaos. The demand for these unique-looking dolls was so high that **parents camped outside stores**, fought in aisles, and even paid outrageous prices just to get one!

14. Which airline innovation, first introduced in the 1980s, allowed passengers to make phone calls from their seats during flights?

a) SkyPhone
b) Airfone
c) FlyTalk
d) JetCom

15. What was the name of the first handheld gaming console with interchangeable cartridges, released in 1989?

a) Atari Lynx
b) Sega Game Gear
c) Nintendo Game Boy
d) TurboExpress

16. The first GPS satellite was launched in the 1980s, laying the foundation for modern navigation systems.

a) True
b) False

17. Which futuristic-looking car, introduced in the early 1980s, became an iconic part of pop culture due to its stainless steel body and gull-wing doors?

a) Pontiac Firebird
b) DeLorean DMC-12
c) Ferrari Testarossa
d) Corvette C4

18. Which airline, founded in 1985, became known for its innovative approach to low-cost air travel and has grown to become one of the world's largest carriers?

a) Southwest Airlines
b) Ryanair
c) Emirates
d) JetBlue

19. The Stealth Bomber, designed to evade radar detection, was first unveiled in the 1980s. What was its official name?

a) F-117 Nighthawk
b) B-2 Spirit
c) F-16 Falcon
d) SR-71 Blackbird

20. What communication breakthrough, introduced in 1983, led to the development of modern cell phone networks?

a) The first text message
b) The 1G cellular network
c) The first fiber-optic cable
d) The invention of voicemail

Sports & Big Achievements

1. Which team won the first Super Bowl of the 1980s (Super Bowl XIV, played in January 1980)?

a) San Francisco 49ers
b) Pittsburgh Steelers
c) Dallas Cowboys
d) Oakland Raiders

2. Who became the youngest heavyweight boxing champion in history when he won the title in 1986?

a) Mike Tyson
b) Evander Holyfield
c) Larry Holmes
d) George Foreman

3. The U.S. boycotted the 1984 Summer Olympics in Los Angeles.

a) True
b) False

4. Which country pulled off one of the biggest upsets in sports history by defeating the Soviet Union in ice hockey at the 1980 Winter Olympics?

a) Canada
b) Finland
c) United States
d) Sweden

5. Who was the first player in NBA history to win three consecutive MVP awards (1984–1986)?

a) Magic Johnson
b) Larry Bird
c) Michael Jordan
d) Kareem Abdul-Jabbar

6. Which legendary female tennis player won all four Grand Slam singles titles in the 1988 season, completing the „Golden Slam"?

a) Chris Evert
b) Martina Navratilova
c) Steffi Graf
d) Billie Jean King

7. The Chicago Bears won their first-ever Super Bowl in the 1980s.

a) True
b) False

8. Which NFL team dominated the second half of the decade, winning back-to-back Super Bowls in 1989 and 1990?

a) San Francisco 49ers
b) New York Giants
c) Denver Broncos
d) Washington Redskins

9. Which sprinter set the world record in the 100m at the 1988 Olympics, only to later be disqualified for doping?

a) Ben Johnson
b) Carl Lewis
c) Linford Christie
d) Calvin Smith

10. Who became the first golfer to win the Masters tournament in back-to-back years (1989, 1990)?

a) Jack Nicklaus
b) Nick Faldo
c) Greg Norman
d) Tom Watson

11. Wayne Gretzky was traded from the Edmonton Oilers to the Los Angeles Kings in the late 1980s.

a) True
b) False

12. Which team won the most NBA championships during the 1980s, capturing five titles?

a) Boston Celtics
b) Los Angeles Lakers
c) Detroit Pistons
d) Philadelphia 76ers

13. What famous horse won the 1989 Kentucky Derby, Preakness Stakes, and Breeders' Cup Classic but missed the Triple Crown after losing the Belmont Stakes?

a) Secretariat
b) Sunday Silence
c) Alysheba
d) Easy Goer

DID YOU KNOW?

The **Nintendo Entertainment System** (NES) launched in the U.S. in **1985**, completely reviving the video game industry after the early '80s crash. **Super Mario Bros.** became a household favorite, turning **Mario** into one of the **most recognizable video game characters** of all time.

14. Which country hosted the 1986 FIFA World Cup, where Diego Maradona delivered his legendary „Hand of God“ goal?

a) Brazil
b) Argentina
c) Spain
d) Mexico

15. John McEnroe and Björn Borg had their last Grand Slam final showdown at the 1981 Wimbledon Championships.

a) True
b) False

16. Which MLB team won the 1986 World Series, with an infamous Game 6 comeback thanks to Bill Buckner's error?

a) New York Mets
b) Boston Red Sox
c) St. Louis Cardinals
d) Los Angeles Dodgers

17. What NBA star set a rookie scoring record in 1984, dropping 63 points in a playoff game against the Boston Celtics?

a) Larry Bird
b) Magic Johnson
c) Michael Jordan
d) Hakeem Olajuwon

18. Who won the 1985 Tour de France, marking the last time a French cyclist would win the event in the 20th century?

a) Greg LeMond
b) Miguel Induráin
c) Bernard Hinault
d) Laurent Fignon

19. Who set the NFL single-season rushing record in 1984 with 2,105 yards, a record that stood for decades?

a) Walter Payton
b) Eric Dickerson
c) Barry Sanders
d) Emmitt Smith

20. Which MLB player became the first to reach 40 home runs and 40 stolen bases in the same season (1988)?

a) Jose Canseco
b) Rickey Henderson
c) Darryl Strawberry
d) Mark McGwire

REMEMBERING THE ELECTRIC '80s!

The 1980s were a decade of **big dreams**, **big hair**, and even **bigger pop culture moments**. It was a time when **cassette tapes** ruled, **arcades** were packed, and **MTV** changed music forever. If you remember jamming to a **boom box**, **recording your favorite songs** off the radio, or **waiting all week for your favorite TV show**, you were living the classic '80s life!

Did you know that in **1981**, the **first space shuttle** blasted off into orbit? Or that in **1989**, the **Berlin Wall** finally **came down**, marking the **end of the Cold War**? The '80s brought us **personal computers**, **camcorders**, **cordless phones**, and the **first mobile phones**, setting the stage for the digital age.

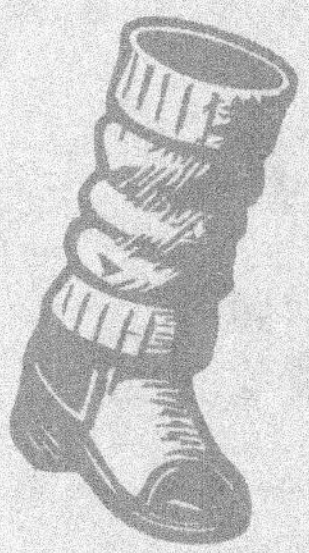

It was also a golden age for entertainment. **Blockbuster movies** like **E.T.**, **Back to the Future**, and **Ghostbusters** kept us glued to the big screen, while **shows** like **The A-Team**, **Cheers**, and **The Golden Girls** had us tuning in every week. And let's not forget the **fashion**! From **neon colors** and **leg warmers** to **Members Only jackets**, **parachute pants**, and **shoulder pads**, style in the '80s was anything but subtle.

Sports fans had their share of unforgettable moments, too, from the **Miracle on Ice** to **Mike Tyson's** dominance in the ring.

Whether you were lacing up roller skates, hitting the arcade, or cheering on your favorite team, the '80s were full of excitement.

Talk & Think About the 1980s

Use these fun questions to spark memories, share stories, and relive what made the '80s so special!

1. What's one thing that immediately reminds you of the '80s? Is it a song, a TV show, a smell, or maybe a place you used to go?

2. Did you have a favorite outfit that screamed '80s fashion? Were you rocking leg warmers, acid-washed jeans, or a classic leather jacket?

3. What was your go-to movie or TV show in the '80s? Did you love action-packed blockbusters, laugh-out-loud sitcoms, or Saturday morning cartoons?

4. Is there a toy or gadget from the '80s that sticks out in your memory? Maybe a Rubik's Cube, an early video game console, or your first camcorder?

5. What kind of music defined the decade for you? Were you blasting glam metal, dancing to pop hits, or grooving to early hip-hop?

6. How did you listen to music in the '80s? Were you making mixtapes on cassette, rocking a Walkman, or collecting vinyl records?

7. Can you think of a major world event from the '80s that made an impact on you? Maybe the fall of the Berlin Wall, Live Aid, or a historic sports moment?

8. What was your weekend routine in the '80s? Was it hanging out at the mall, going to the movies, roller-skating, or heading to an arcade?

9. What was your first experience with a computer like? Did you use an Apple II, play early video games, or marvel at the power of a floppy disk?

10. If you could relive one moment from the '80s, what would it be and why?

Write About the 1980s

Take a moment to jot down your favorite memories from the '80s. Maybe it was the first time you saw Michael Jackson moonwalk, your first car, your first concert, or the thrill of watching your favorite team win a championship.

The '80s were a time of bold style, unforgettable music, groundbreaking technology, and culture-defining moments. If you were rocking out at a concert, making calls on a giant cordless phone, or watching history unfold on the evening news, your stories are part of what made this decade so iconic!

CHAPTER FIVE

The 1990s

Ah, the 1990s! A decade of **dial-up internet**, **blockbuster movies**, **iconic TV shows**, and **music** that still makes us turn up the volume. It was the era of **grunge** and **gangsta rap**, **boy bands** and **pop divas**, the **Macarena** and **MTV's TRL**. Whether you were blasting **Nirvana's** "Smells Like Teen Spirit," dancing to **MC Hammer's** "U Can't Touch This," or singing along to the **Backstreet Boys'** "I Want It That Way," the '90s had a soundtrack for everyone.

Movies were bigger than ever, with **Titanic**, **Jurassic Park**, and **The Lion King** dominating the **box office**. And let's not forget the **TV shows**! Whether you were laughing at **Friends**, solving mysteries with **The X-Files**, or watching **Will Smith** rule as **The Fresh Prince of Bel-Air**, there was always something worth staying up for.

Technology took a huge leap, too. The '90s gave us **Windows 95**, the rise of the **Internet**, **Tamagotchis**, and **flip phones**. Who could forget the frustration of **waiting for a webpage to load** or the agony of **someone picking up the phone** while you were trying to **connect to AOL**?

And, of course, **fashion** had its own vibe, too! **Baggy jeans**, **butterfly clips**, **flannel shirts**, and **platform sneakers** were all the rage. You might have been rocking a **choker necklace**, wearing **JNCO jeans**, or collecting **Beanie Babies**, and if you were, then you were part of a decade that defined cool in its own way.

Let's pop in a mixtape and get ready to revisit the decade of Game Boys, Blockbuster nights, and the unforgettable Y2K panic!

Daily Life & Childhood Memories

1. What was the name of the popular stuffed toy line that became a massive collecting craze in the '90s?

a) Beanie Babies
b) Furby
c) Cabbage Patch Kids
d) Tamagotchi

2. Which writing tool became a classroom favorite in the '90s, known for its smooth ink and vibrant colors?

a) Milky Pens
b) Gel Pens
c) Felt-Tip Markers
d) Highlighters

3. Goosebumps books were one of the best-selling children's book series of the 1990s.

a) True
b) False

4. What color were the original Game Boy screens when powered on?

a) Black and white
b) Green and black
c) Blue and gray
d) Red and black

5. Which of these shoes was a must-have fashion trend in the '90s?

a) Ugg boots
b) Heelys
c) Doc Martens
d) Crocs

6. Which electronic pet toy, released in 1997, required kids to „feed" and care for it?

a) Giga Pet
b) Digimon
c) Furby
d) Tamagotchi

7. „Macarena" by Los Del Rio was the longest-running No. 1 hit of the 1990s.

a) True
b) False

The **first-ever website** went live in **1991**, marking the **beginning** of the **World Wide Web** and forever changing how people communicated, shopped, and searched for information.

8. What was the most common way kids watched movies at home in the early '90s?

a) DVD
b) LaserDisc
c) VHS tapes
d) Streaming services

9. What popular fruit-flavored candy came in little plastic containers shaped like barrels or tubes and required squeezing to get the candy out?

a) Gushers
b) Fruit Roll-Ups
c) Squeeze Pops
d) Push Pop

10. What type of pants became a signature look for skaters, ravers, and hip-hop fans in the late '90s?

a) Skinny jeans
b) JNCO jeans
c) Cargo pants
d) Corduroys

11. Lisa Frank's colorful school supplies were mostly targeted at teenage boys.

a) True
b) False

12. What snack food, introduced in the '90s, was known for its unusual neon-colored dipping sauces, including blue and pink frosting?

a) Gushers
b) Dunkaroos
c) Fruit by the Foot
d) Lunchables

13. What 1990s TV show featured kids competing in temple-themed obstacle courses, facing the dreaded „Temple Guards"?

a) Double Dare
b) Guts
c) Legends of the Hidden Temple
d) Are You Afraid of the Dark?

14. Which fashion accessory became a classroom fad and was later banned in some schools due to safety concerns?

a) Mood rings
b) Snap bracelets
c) Choker necklaces
d) Slap watches

15. „Boy Meets World“ was a spin-off of „Saved by the Bell.“

a) True
b) False

16. What candy was marketed with the tagline „Taste the Rainbow“?

a) Starburst
b) Skittles
c) Airheads
d) Nerds

17. Which Nickelodeon game show slimed its contestants and made messy obstacle courses famous?

a) Figure It Out
b) What Would You Do?
c) Wild & Crazy Kids
d) Double Dare

18. What was the name of the handheld electronic device that allowed users to exchange messages before cell phones became common?

a) PalmPilot
b) Blackberry
c) Pocket Messenger
d) Pager

19. What was the name of the binder-based organizer system that kids and teens used to collect and trade stickers, photos, and magazine cutouts?

a) Sticker Book
b) Scrapbook
c) Smashbook
d) Slam Book

20. What was the name of the iconic inflatable furniture trend that was popular for bedrooms and playrooms in the late '90s?

a) Bubble Chairs
b) Bean Bag Loungers
c) Inflatable Chairs
d) Air Couches

Entertainment & Culture

1. What was the first animated film to be nominated for Best Picture at the Academy Awards?

a) The Lion King
b) Toy Story
c) Beauty and the Beast
d) Aladdin

2. Which TV series finale in 1998 became one of the most-watched episodes in television history?

a) Seinfeld
b) Friends
c) Cheers
d) The X-Files

3. The first book in the Harry Potter series was released in the United States before the UK.

a) True
b) False

4. What was the name of the dance craze that took over in the mid-1990s, thanks to a hit song by Los Del Rio?

a) The Running Man
b) The Macarena
c) The Cha Cha Slide
d) The Electric Slide

5. Which boy band released the hit single 'I Want It That Way' in 1999?

a) *NSYNC
b) 98 Degrees
c) New Kids on the Block
d) Backstreet Boys

6. What popular 1990s sitcom followed six friends living in New York City?

a) Will & Grace
b) Friends
c) Dawson's Creek
d) Saved by the Bell

7. The Spice Girls' real names were Posh, Sporty, Scary, Baby, and Ginger.

a) True
b) False

DID YOU KNOW?

By the **mid-'90s, Beanie Babies** were everywhere. People treated them like **investments**, believing they'd be worth a fortune in the future. Some rare editions did **sell for thousands**, but when the fad ended, so did their value.

8. What was the highest-grossing movie of the 1990s?

a) Jurassic Park
b) Titanic
c) The Lion King
d) The Matrix

9. Which grunge band, led by Kurt Cobain, helped define the sound of the early 1990s?

a) Pearl Jam
b) Soundgarden
c) Nirvana
d) Alice in Chains

10. Which catchphrase was made famous by Budweiser's 1999 commercial?

a) "You got it, dude!"
b) "Whassup?"
c) "Talk to the hand."
d) "Bada bing, bada boom!"

11. „The Fresh Prince of Bel-Air" was Will Smith's first acting role.

a) True
b) False

12. Which female artist's 1995 song „You Oughta Know" became an instant hit and helped define the rise of alternative rock in the '90s?

a) Fiona Apple
b) Sheryl Crow
c) Alanis Morissette
d) Jewel

13. Which fashion trend became wildly popular in the 1990s, thanks to hip-hop and streetwear culture?

a) Bell-bottoms
b) Baggy jeans
c) Popped collars
d) Capri pants

14. Who starred as the title character in the 1990 film Edward Scissorhands?

a) Brad Pitt
b) Leonardo DiCaprio
c) Johnny Depp
d) Keanu Reeves

15. Tamagotchis were originally designed as a learning tool for children before becoming a global toy craze.

a) True
b) False

16. What iconic MTV show, first airing in 1992, was known for following strangers living together in a house?

a) Punk'd
b) Jackass
c) The Real World
d) Road Rules

17. Which famous rapper's album, The Marshall Mathers LP, made him a household name in the late '90s?

a) Tupac Shakur
b) Jay-Z
c) Eminem
d) Snoop Dogg

18. What was the name of the fictional town in Twin Peaks, the hit mystery TV show from the early '90s?

a) Riverdale
b) Twin Peaks
c) Mystic Falls
d) Roswell

19. Which animated TV show, debuting in 1997, became one of the longest-running and most controversial adult cartoons in history?

a) Beavis and Butt-Head
b) South Park
c) The Simpsons
d) Family Guy

20. What 1990s Disney movie featured a young lion cub who learns to take his place as king?

a) Hercules
b) Mulan
c) The Lion King
d) Pocahontas

Historical Events & Headlines

1. In 1991, what major event marked the official end of the Cold War?

a) The reunification of Germany
b) The signing of the START treaty
c) The collapse of the Soviet Union
d) The fall of the Berlin Wall

2. What was the major international agreement signed in 1993 that created the world's largest free trade zone?

a) NAFTA
b) NATO Expansion Act
c) The Kyoto Protocol
d) The European Union Treaty

3. Nelson Mandela was elected as South Africa's first Black president in the early 1990s.

a) True
b) False

4. What former football star and actor was at the center of the most famous criminal trial of the 1990s?

a) Mike Tyson
b) Dennis Rodman
c) O.J. Simpson
d) Ray Lewis

5. In 1994, what country experienced a devastating genocide that led to the deaths of an estimated 800,000 people?

a) Bosnia
b) Somalia
c) Rwanda
d) Sudan

6. What was the new European currency introduced in 1999 that aimed to unify the continent's economy?

a) Franc
b) Euro
c) Pound Sterling
d) Deutsche Mark

7. The World Trade Organization (WTO) was officially established in 1995.

a) True
b) False

DID YOU KNOW?

At its peak in **1994**, **Blockbuster Video** had **over 4,000 stores worldwide**, making Friday night movie rentals a cherished tradition before streaming services took over.

8. What international event in 1997 was watched by an estimated 2.5 billion people worldwide?

a) The Hong Kong handover to China
b) The Mars Pathfinder landing
c) The funeral of Princess Diana
d) The release of Titanic

9. In 1992, riots broke out in Los Angeles following the acquittal of police officers in the beating of what man?

a) Rodney King
b) Amadou Diallo
c) Trayvon Martin
d) James Byrd Jr.

10. What was the name of the territory handed back to China by the British in 1997?

a) Taiwan
b) Macau
c) Hong Kong
d) Singapore

11. In 1999, NATO launched airstrikes against Serbia to stop the ethnic cleansing of Albanians in Kosovo.

a) True
b) False

12. In 1993, U.S. federal agents engaged in a deadly 51-day standoff with members of what religious sect in Waco, Texas?

a) Heaven's Gate
b) The Branch Davidians
c) The People's Temple
d) The Fundamentalist LDS Church

13. What global environmental agreement, signed in 1997, aimed to reduce greenhouse gas emissions?

a) The Paris Agreement
b) The Rio Summit
c) The Kyoto Protocol
d) The Montreal Accord

14. In what year did the United Kingdom and Ireland sign the Good Friday Agreement, bringing peace to Northern Ireland?

a) 1990
b) 1995
c) 1998
d) 1999

15. The Y2K crisis, which caused panic about computers failing at the turn of the century, resulted in widespread system failures.

a) True
b) False

16. Who became the first female U.S. Secretary of State in 1997?

a) Hillary Clinton
b) Condoleezza Rice
c) Madeleine Albright
d) Janet Reno

17. What 1995 event was the deadliest act of domestic terrorism in U.S. history at the time?

a) The Atlanta Olympic bombing
b) The Oklahoma City bombing
c) The Columbine shooting
d) The Unabomber attacks

18. In 1998, which U.S. president was impeached by the House of Representatives?

a) George H.W. Bush
b) Bill Clinton
c) Ronald Reagan
d) George W. Bush

19. In the 1990s, NASA successfully cloned the first mammal, a sheep named Dolly.

a) True
b) False

20. In 1991, the U.S. and allied forces launched Operation Desert Storm to remove the military of what country from Kuwait?

a) Syria
b) Iran
c) Iraq
d) Libya

Technology & Innovation

1. What was the name of the first web browser, launched in 1993, that helped bring the Internet to the public?

a) Netscape Navigator
b) Internet Explorer
c) Mosaic
d) Firefox

2. Which gaming console, released in 1994, became one of the best-selling of all time?

a) Nintendo 64
b) Sega Dreamcast
c) PlayStation
d) Xbox

3. The first-ever text message (SMS) was sent in the 1990s.

a) True
b) False

4. **What device, introduced in 1998, revolutionized music by allowing users to store and play digital music files?**

   a) MP3 player
   b) Walkman
   c) MiniDisc player
   d) CD player

5. **Which web-based email service, launched in 1996, helped popularize checking email from any computer with an Internet connection?**

   a) Gmail
   b) Hotmail
   c) Yahoo Mail
   d) AOL Mail

6. **What was the name of the operating system Microsoft released in 1995, which introduced the Start menu?**

   a) Windows 3.1
   b) Windows 95
   c) Windows XP
   d) Windows NT

7. Google was founded in 1998 as a search engine project by two Stanford students.

a) True
b) False

8. Which transportation breakthrough was introduced in 1994, allowing people to use electronic toll collection on highways?

a) FasTrak
b) EZ-Pass
c) AutoPay
d) SmartTag

9. What was the name of the space telescope launched in 1990 that revolutionized astronomy?

a) Kepler Space Telescope
b) Spitzer Space Telescope
c) Hubble Space Telescope
d) Voyager II

10. In 1995, which online retail company was founded, initially selling books before expanding into a global marketplace?

a) eBay
b) Amazon
c) Google
d) PayPal

11. The first DVD players were released in the 1990s, replacing VHS as the dominant home video format.

a) True
b) False

12. Which popular portable gaming device, released in 1998, allowed players to battle and trade virtual creatures?

a) Game Boy Color
b) Neo Geo Pocket
c) Sega Game Gear
d) PlayStation Portable

13. What communication device became widely used in the 1990s, allowing people to send short text messages before cell phones were common?

a) Beeper
b) Two-Way Radio
c) Blackberry
d) Pocket Messenger

In **1996**, the **Tamagotchi** became a global phenomenon. Kids (and adults) everywhere were **obsessed** with feeding, cleaning, and playing with their tiny virtual pets—if they didn't forget to check on them, that is!

14. The Mars Pathfinder, which landed on Mars in 1997, was the first spacecraft to successfully reach another planet.

a) True
b) False

15. In 1993, which company introduced the Pentium processor, significantly advancing personal computing power?

a) IBM
b) Intel
c) Apple
d) AMD

16. What popular online auction site, launched in 1995, changed the way people bought and sold goods online?

a) Craigslist
b) Amazon
c) eBay
d) Yahoo! Auctions

17. Which technology, first demonstrated in 1996, became the foundation for modern smartphone touchscreens?

a) Resistive touchscreens
b) Capacitive touchscreens
c) Optical trackpads
d) Stylus input

18. In 1999, NASA lost contact with which space probe due to a mix-up between metric and imperial measurement systems?

a) Mars Pathfinder
b) Mars Climate Orbiter
c) Cassini-Huygens
d) Voyager I

19. Wi-Fi technology was first introduced to consumers in the 1990s.

a) True
b) False

20. What car safety feature, introduced in the 1990s, became a standard in many vehicles to prevent skidding?

a) Electronic Stability Control (ESC)
b) Adaptive Cruise Control
c) Lane Departure Warning
d) Parking Sensors

Sports & Big Achievements

1. Which country won the first-ever FIFA Women's World Cup in 1991?

a) United States
b) Germany
c) Brazil
d) Norway

2. In 1997, who became the youngest golfer to win The Masters at just 21 years old?

a) Phil Mickelson
b) Tiger Woods
c) Ernie Els
d) Vijay Singh

3. The 1992 „Dream Team," featuring Michael Jordan and Magic Johnson, lost a game in the Barcelona Olympics.

a) True
b) False

4. What NBA team won six championships in the 1990s, cementing their dominance?

a) Los Angeles Lakers
b) Houston Rockets
c) Chicago Bulls
d) San Antonio Spurs

5. In 1999, who became the first female soccer player to appear on the cover of Sports Illustrated after leading the U.S. Women's National Team to World Cup victory?

a) Mia Hamm
b) Brandi Chastain
c) Julie Foudy
d) Kristine Lilly

6. What NFL team won back-to-back Super Bowls in 1997 and 1998, led by quarterback John Elway?

a) Dallas Cowboys
b) Green Bay Packers
c) Denver Broncos
d) San Francisco 49ers

7. In 1994, Major League Baseball (MLB) had a season without a World Series due to a player strike.

a) True
b) False

8. Who won seven Formula 1 World Championships, with two of them occurring in the 1990s?

a) Ayrton Senna
b) Mika Häkkinen
c) Michael Schumacher
d) Damon Hill

9. In 1998, which NHL team won its first Stanley Cup, completing a four-game sweep in the Finals?

a) Detroit Red Wings
b) Dallas Stars
c) Colorado Avalanche
d) New Jersey Devils

10. Which heavyweight boxing match in 1997 ended with a shocking ear-biting incident?

a) Evander Holyfield vs. George Foreman
b) Mike Tyson vs. Evander Holyfield
c) Lennox Lewis vs. Mike Tyson
d) Riddick Bowe vs. Evander Holyfield

11. The 1999 UEFA Champions League Final ended with Manchester United scoring two goals in injury time to win the trophy.

a) True
b) False

12. **What record-setting sprinter became the first athlete to win back-to-back Olympic gold medals in the 100m and 200m at both the 1992 and 1996 Olympics?**

a) Michael Johnson
b) Donovan Bailey
c) Maurice Greene
d) Carl Lewis

13. **Which team won the first-ever BCS National Championship Game in college football in 1998?**

a) Nebraska
b) Florida State
c) Tennessee
d) Michigan

As the year **2000** approached, the **Y2K panic** had the world in chaos. Many feared that **computers wouldn't recognize the year „00,"** leading to massive system failures—but when midnight struck, everything was just fine.

14. Who became the first female driver to lead a lap in the Indianapolis 500, achieving the feat in 1992?

a) Janet Guthrie
b) Lyn St. James
c) Sarah Fisher
d) Danica Patrick

15. The 1994 FIFA World Cup Final, held in the United States, ended in a penalty shootout for the first time in history.

a) True
b) False

16. Which tennis player dominated the 1990s, winning 14 Grand Slam singles titles, including seven at Wimbledon?

a) Pete Sampras
b) Andre Agassi
c) Boris Becker
d) Roger Federer

17. Who became the first African American to win a Grand Slam singles title in the Open Era when she won the 1999 U.S. Open?

a) Serena Williams
b) Venus Williams
c) Althea Gibson
d) Jennifer Capriati

18. Which baseball player broke Roger Maris' single-season home run record in 1998?

a) Mark McGwire
b) Barry Bonds
c) Sammy Sosa
d Ken Griffey Jr.

19. In 1991, who became the first openly HIV-positive athlete to retire from professional sports?

a) Arthur Ashe
b) Magic Johnson
c) Greg Louganis
d) Bo Jackson

20. The 1996 Atlanta Olympics were the first to feature professional baseball players.

a) True
b) False

REMEMBERING THE TOTALLY '90s!

The 1990s were a decade of **fast-changing trends**, unforgettable **pop culture**, and **technology** that **shaped the future**. It was a time when the **Internet** was still a mystery, **pagers** were the height of communication, and **video rental stores** were the go-to for movie night. If you ever **waited** 10 minutes **for a song to download**, carried a **Discman** that skipped with every step, or collected **Beanie Babies** like they were gold, you were living the ultimate '90s experience!

Did you know that in **1991**, the **World Wide Web** was launched, changing the way we connect forever? Or that in **1999**, the world panicked over **Y2K**, fearing computers would stop working at midnight? The '90s also gave us **Google**, **DVDs**, and the **first-ever text message**. These innovations still impact our lives today.

Entertainment was bigger than ever. **Blockbusters** like **Titanic**, **Jurassic Park**, and **The Matrix** ruled the box office, while **TV classics** like **Friends**, **The Fresh Prince of Bel-Air**, and **The X-Files** kept us glued to the screen. And let's not forget the **music**! Whether you were rocking out to **Nirvana**, dancing to the **Spice Girls**, or belting out a **Backstreet Boys** ballad, the '90s had a sound for everyone.

Sports fans had plenty of reasons to cheer, from **Michael Jordan** leading the Bulls to **six NBA titles** to the **U.S. Women's National Team** winning the **World Cup** in **1999**. And who could forget the iconic moment when **Brandi Chastain** celebrated with her famous **jersey toss**?

Whether you were hanging out at the mall, battling on a Nintendo 64, or rushing to answer your landline before the answering machine kicked in, the '90s were filled with experiences that still bring a smile today.

Talk & Think About the 1990s

Use these fun questions to relive the '90s, share your memories, and spark some nostalgia!

1. What's the first thing that comes to mind when you think of the '90s? Is it a song, a fashion trend, or a favorite hangout spot?

2. Did you have a signature '90s fashion statement? Were you rocking JNCO jeans, butterfly clips, platform sneakers, or a Starter jacket?

3. What was your go-to '90s movie or TV show? Did you love a good rom-com, an action-packed thriller, or a Nickelodeon cartoon?

4. Is there a gadget or technology from the '90s that you remember? Maybe your first cell phone, a Tamagotchi, or an AOL dial-up connection?

5. What kind of music defined the decade for you? Were you into grunge, pop, rap, R&B, or alternative rock?

6. How did you spend your weekends in the '90s? Were you at the mall, hitting up a concert, renting movies, or trading Pokémon cards?

7. Can you think of a major world event from the '90s that had a lasting impact on you? Maybe the O.J. Simpson trial, the rise of the Internet, or the excitement of Y2K?

8. What was your first experience with online culture? Did you join AOL chat rooms, create a Geocities website, or send your first email?

9. If you could relive one day in the '90s, what would it be and why?

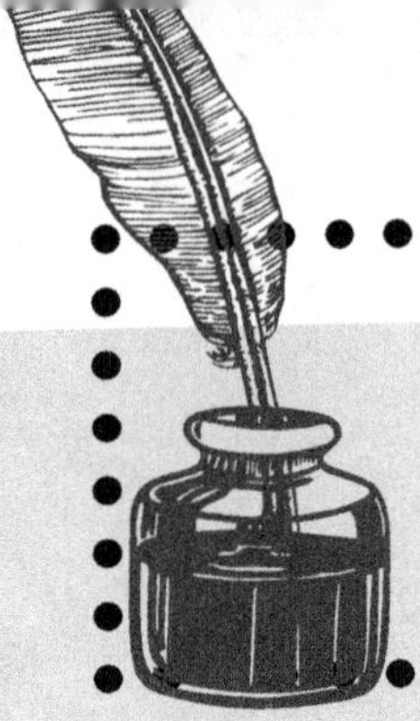

Write About the 1990s

Take a moment to jot down your favorite '90s memories. Maybe it was getting your first car, recording the perfect mixtape, attending a concert, or experiencing the excitement of the new millennium approaching.

The '90s were a time of innovation, unforgettable entertainment, and trends that still make us smile today. Whether you were laughing at sitcoms, making the most of your Blockbuster membership, or rushing home to catch TRL, your stories are part of what made this decade so memorable. Let's keep the nostalgia alive!

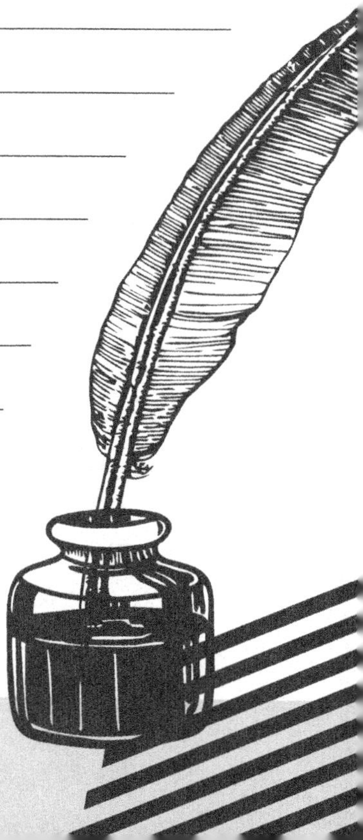

A TRIP DOWN MEMORY LANE

Cherishing the Past and Sharing the Stories that Make You—You!

From **sock hops** and **soda fountains** to **boom boxes** and **beepers**, we've traveled through **five incredible decades**, each packed with **unforgettable moments**, **groundbreaking inventions**, and **cultural shifts** that shaped the world. Whether you were dancing to **Elvis** in the **'50s**, cruising to **The Beatles** in the **'60s**, rocking **bell-bottoms** in the **'70s**, blasting **cassettes** in the **'80s**, or logging onto the **Internet** for the first time in the **'90s**, every era has left its mark.

But this book isn't just about trivia—it's about

memories, **laughter**, and **connection**. Maybe a question reminded you of your **childhood home**, a **favorite vacation**, or the **first time you held a record** in your hands. Perhaps you found yourself **sharing a story** with a **grandchild**, **reminiscing** with an **old friend**, or simply **smiling** as you thought back to the **good old days**.

No matter how much time passes, our **memories are treasures** that **deserve to be shared**. So keep the stories alive! **Talk** about them, **write** them down, and **relive** them with those you love. Because while time moves forward, the joy of looking back never fades.

Here's to the past, the laughter, and the moments that make life unforgettable!

ANSWER KEY

The 1950s

DAILY LIFE & CHILDHOOD MEMORIES

1. **b)** Vinyl records
2. **c)** Barbie
3. **b)** Coca-Cola
4. **b)** The Mickey Mouse Club
5. **b)** Poodle cut
6. **b)** False – The first Barbie doll was released in 1959.
7. **b)** Duz
8. **b)** Electric blender
9. **a)** Iceboxes
10. **c)** Risk
11. **c)** Dacron
12. **b)** RCA
13. **a)** Trix
14. **b)** Gas
15. **b)** TV dinners
16. **a)** Writing lines on the chalkboard
17. **a)** Cruiser bike
18. **b)** Silly Putty
19. **d)** All of the above
20. **a)** Tupperware

ENTERTAINMENT & CULTURE

1. **b)** I Love Lucy
2. **a)** Casablanca
3. **a)** Pink
4. **c)** Cinderella
5. **b)** Catcher in the Rye
6. **b)** Natalie Wood
7. **b)** The Cleavers
8. **d)** Suede loafers
9. **d)** Bwana Devil
10. **b)** Neat-o

11. a) True
12. a) Clayton Moore
13. c) C-57D
14. c) Charlton Heston
15. b) False
16. a) The Amos 'n' Andy Show
17. b) Chuck Berry
18. c) Disneyland
19. a) Ben-Hur
20. b) Buddy Holly

HISTORICAL EVENTS & HEADLINES

1. b) Korean War
2. b) Dwight D. Eisenhower
3. b) Sputnik 1
4. b) False - The Civil Rights Act was signed into law on July 2nd, 1964
5. a) Warsaw Pact
6. d) Hawaii's Statehood
7. a) Polio vaccine
8. c) U-2 Spy Plane Incident
9. c) Brown v. Board of Education
10. a) True
11. b) NASA
12. b) 1952
13. c) Cuba
14. c) Veterans Day
15. a) True
16. a) Rosa Parks
17. c) Nikita Khrushchev
18. c) Mount Everest
19. c) Operation Castle
20. a) True

TECHNOLOGY & INNOVATION

1. d) Diners Club
2. a) Pacemaker
3. a) True – The first color TV broadcast occurred in the U.S. in 1951.

4. b) Nuclear fusion
5. a) Seat belts
6. b) Microwave oven
7. c) De Havilland Comet
8. a) Transistor
9. b) False – The first satellite, Sputnik 1, was launched by the Soviet Union in 1957, not the United States.
10. b) Fender
11. c) Atlas
12. b) Refrigerator with automatic defrost
13. a) Plate tectonics
14. a) True – The first video game, Tennis for Two, was created in 1958 by physicist William Higinbotham.
15. c) Oldsmobile Rocket 88
16. c) Transatlantic telephone cable
17. b) True – The first man-made object to reach the Moon was Luna 2, launched by the Soviet Union in 1959.
18. b) Television
19. a) Sony
20. b) Ultrasound

SPORTS & BIG ACHIEVEMENTS

1. b) Brooklyn Dodgers
2. c) Rocky Marciano
3. a) True – The first NBA All-Star Game was played on March 2, 1951, in Boston, Massachusetts.
4. b) Formula One World Championship
5. a) Run a sub-4-minute mile
6. c) Finland
7. a) Ken Rosewall
8. a) True
9. d) Arnold Palmer
10. a) Soviet invasion of Hungary
11. c) Boston Celtics
12. b) False – The first televised college football game was actually in 1939, between Fordham and Waynesburg.

13. **b)** Althea Gibson
14. **b)** Citation
15. **c)** 7
16. **b)** Bob Cousy
17. **a)** True – The 1954 FIFA World Cup was held in Switzerland, the first since World War II.
18. **a)** Sugar Ray Robinson vs. Jake LaMotta VI
19. **c)** Montreal Canadiens
20. **b)** Tenley Albright

The 1960s

DAILY LIFE & CHILDHOOD MEMORIES

1. **c)** Creepy Crawlers
2. **b)** Mr. Ed
3. **b)** Polyester
4. **c)** Mini skirt
5. **b)** Cap'n Crunch
6. **d)** Color television
7. **b)** Starburst
8. **b)** False – Bicycle helmets were not widely used until decades later. Most kids rode without them.
9. **c)** Operation
10. **c)** Pillbox hat
11. **c)** Plastic
12. **b)** False – The transistor radio was actually introduced in the 1950s, but it became extremely popular among teenagers in the 1960s.
13. **c)** Felt-tip markers
14. **d)** All of the above
15. **a)** Frisbee
16. **b)** False – Remote controls were rare, and most TVs were still manually operated.

17. **b)** Paisley

18. **b)** Hot Wheels

19. **a)** Where the Wild Things Are

20. **b)** Burger King

ENTERTAINMENT & CULTURE

1. **b)** I Want to Hold Your Hand

2. **c)** The Blue Meanies

3. **a)** True – The Sound of Music (1965) was the highest-grossing film of the decade, surpassing Gone with the Wind in total revenue.

4. **b)** Star Trek

5. **b)** The Twist

6. **b)** To Kill a Mockingbird

7. **b)** Aretha Franklin

8. **a)** True – The Flintstones (1960) was the first animated series to air during prime-time television.

9. **b)** „That's one small step for man, one giant leap for mankind."

10. **b)** Sean Connery

11. **b)** Mary Quant

12. **b)** False – The original Batman TV series was campy and humorous, often using exaggerated sound effects and colorful visuals.

13. **d)** (I Can't Get No) Satisfaction

14. **b)** 2001: A Space Odyssey

15. **b)** The Brady Bunch

16. **c)** The Temptations

17. **a)** True – The term „hippie" became widely used in the 1960s, particularly associated with the counterculture movement in Haight-Ashbury, San Francisco.

18. **c)** Steve McQueen

19. **c)** Woodstock

20. **b)** Sesame Street

HISTORICAL EVENTS & HEADLINES

1. **b)** Assassination of John F. Kennedy
2. **c)** East Germany
3. **a)** True – The Civil Rights Act of 1964 legally ended segregation and outlawed discrimination based on race, color, religion, sex, or national origin.
4. **b)** „I Have a Dream"
5. **b)** Vietnam War
6. **c)** Yuri Gagarin
7. **b)** Cuban Missile Crisis
8. **b)** False – John F. Kennedy won the 1960 election, defeating Richard Nixon. Nixon later won in 1968.
9. **a)** Monterey Pop Festival
10. **c)** Kenya
11. **b)** Apollo 11
12. **b)** False – The Bay of Pigs invasion was a failed U.S.-backed attempt to overthrow Fidel Castro.
13. **b)** Robert F. Kennedy
14. **b)** Summer Olympics
15. **b)** The peace sign
16. **a)** Earl Warren
17. **a)** True – The Beatles' last public concert was at Candlestick Park, San Francisco, on August 29, 1966.
18. **b)** The Feminine Mystique
19. **a)** Operation Rolling Thunder
20. **b)** South Africa

TECHNOLOGY & INNOVATION

1. **a)** Artificial hip replacement
2. **a)** Bullet train (Shinkansen)
3. **a)** True – The first successful human heart transplant was performed in 1967 by Dr. Christiaan Barnard in South Africa.

4. **c)** COBOL
5. **b)** Apollo 8
6. **c)** 8-track tape
7. **b)** False – The first ATM was installed in London, UK, in 1967; the U.S. followed later.
8. **b)** Telstar
9. **b)** Concorde
10. **b)** Douglas Engelbart
11. **b)** CT scanning
12. **a)** True – The Boeing 747 was introduced in 1969, revolutionizing air travel.
13. **b)** Lunar Rover
14. **a)** Self-cleaning oven
15. **a)** Microchip
16. **a)** True – The first video game console, The Brown Box, was invented by Ralph Baer in 1967.
17. **b)** Weather satellite
18. **b)** Cosmic microwave background radiation
19. **b)** Seat belts
20. **b)** Hubble Space Telescope

SPORTS & BIG ACHIEVEMENTS

1. **b)** Roy Emerson
2. **c)** England
3. **b)** False – Muhammad Ali won his first heavyweight title in 1964 when he defeated Sonny Liston.
4. **a)** NFL-AFL Championship Game
5. **b)** 100
6. **a)** Jim Clark
7. **b)** False – The 1964 Summer Olympics were held in Tokyo, while Mexico City hosted in 1968.
8. **a)** Charlie Sifford
9. **c)** New York Yankees
10. **b)** Wilma Rudolph
11. **a)** True – The Green Bay Packers won the first two Super Bowls in 1967 and 1968 under coach Vince Lombardi.

12. c) Muhammad Ali
13. a) Northern Dancer
14. b) Arnold Palmer
15. a) True – The 1968 Olympics in Mexico City introduced an all-weather synthetic track for the first time.
16. d) Kansas City Athletics
17. a) Alabama
18. a) Judo
19. b) Wilt Chamberlain
20. b) It set a world record that lasted for 23 years

The 1970s

DAILY LIFE & CHILDHOOD MEMORIES

1. a) Fisher-Price Little People
2. a) Polyester
3. a) True – The Rubik's Cube was invented in 1974 by Ernő Rubik.
4. b) Scratch 'n Sniff Stickers
5. c) Hostess Ding Dongs
6. b) 8-Track Player
7. a) True – The TV dinner gained massive popularity in the 1970s as families sought convenience meals.
8. c) Pay Day
9. a) The Brady Bunch
10. a) Platform shoes
11. a) True – The Atari 2600 was released in 1977.
12. a) Writing sentences
13. a) Lava lamp
14. a) Pet Rock
15. a) True – Schoolhouse Rock! debuted in 1973.
16. c) Feathered hair
17. d) Spin Art
18. c) Cup Noodles

19. a) True – Skateboarding exploded in popularity thanks to polyurethane wheels.

20. c) Mood Ring

ENTERTAINMENT & CULTURE

1. b) Happy Days

2. a) „You talkin' to me?"

3. a) True – Rocky was released in 1976 and became an instant classic.

4. b) Donna Summer

5. b) Star Wars

6. c) Johnny Carson

7. a) True – The phrase „May the Force be with you" became iconic after the release of Star Wars in 1977.

8. b) The Eagles

9. c) Carrie Fisher

10. b) Platform shoes

11. a) False – The Brady Bunch premiered in 1969 but ran primarily through the 1970s, making it a classic show of the decade.

12. c) Stephen King's horror novels

13. b) The Hustle

14. b) John Travolta

15. a) True – The Sony Walkman debuted in 1979, revolutionizing personal music listening.

16. c) Scooby-Doo, Where Are You!

17. a) John Travolta

18. a) Good Times

19. a) True – Ziggy Stardust, David Bowie's iconic alter ego, was introduced in 1972.

20. d) M*A*S*H

HISTORICAL EVENTS & HEADLINES

1. b) Gerald Ford
2. b) Vietnam War
3. b) False – Nixon resigned before he could be impeached.
4. a) China
5. a) New York
6. c) Leonid Brezhnev
7. a) True – The U.S. celebrated its 200th anniversary in 1976.
8. a) Angola
9. b) Camp David Accords
10. b) The Shah of Iran
11. a) True – The first Earth Day was held on April 22, 1970.
12. b) Three Mile Island
13. c) Greenpeace
14. b) Richard Nixon
15. b) False – The ERA was passed by Congress in 1972 but was never ratified by enough states.
16. b) Summer Olympics in Munich
17. c) First successful Mars landing
18. b) Harold Wilson
19. a) True – The Concorde entered service in 1976.
20. c) Watergate

TECHNOLOGY & INNOVATION

1. c) MITS
2. b) CT scan
3. a) True – The first email was sent by Ray Tomlinson in 1971.
4. a) Cassette tape
5. c) Magnavox
6. c) Salyut 1
7. a) True – The first mobile phone call was made by Martin Cooper in 1973.
8. b) Viking 1
9. a) LCD
10. b) Apple

11. **a)** True – The first barcode scanner was used in a grocery store in 1974.
12. **b)** VHS
13. **a)** The OPEC Oil Embargo
14. **c)** Microvision
15. **b)** False – The first artificial heart was implanted in the 1980s, not the 1970s.
16. **b)** Space Shuttle
17. **b)** Texas Instruments
18. **b)** False – GPS was initially developed for military use in the 1970s and later adapted for civilians.
19. **b)** Honda Civic
20. **c)** Floppy Disk

SPORTS & BIG ACHIEVEMENTS

1. **c)** Brazil
2. **a)** Secretariat
3. **d)** None—no team won three in a row
4. **a)** True – Nadia Comaneci scored the first perfect 10 in Olympic history at the 1976 Games.
5. **d)** Bobby Riggs
6. **a)** Arthur Ashe
7. **a)** False – Women's basketball made its Olympic debut in 1976.
8. **c)** Miami Dolphins
9. **a)** Oscar Robertson
10. **b)** False – Muhammad Ali won the „Rumble in the Jungle“ against George Foreman.
11. **b)** The Soviet Union controversially defeated the U.S. in the final seconds
12. **b)** Oakland Athletics
13. **c)** Portland Trail Blazers
14. **b)** False – Jack Nicklaus won multiple major titles but never all four in one year.
15. **a)** Montreal
16. **c)** Kareem Abdul-Jabbar

17. **d)** Mark Spitz
18. **b)** False – No female driver won the Indianapolis 500 in the 1970s.
19. **a)** Montreal Canadiens
20. **a)** Pete Rose

The 1980s

DAILY LIFE & CHILDHOOD MEMORIES

1. **b)** Cabbage Patch Kids
2. **c)** Flannel shirts
3. **a)** True – Some schools banned Trapper Keepers because teachers found them too bulky and distracting in class.
4. **c)** Stinky Stickers
5. **b)** Cassette tapes
6. **c)** Commodore 64
7. **b)** False – Happy Meals were first introduced in 1979.
8. **b)** Skip-It
9. **b)** New Coke
10. **b)** Lite-Brite
11. **a)** True – 1-900 numbers were popular in the '80s, and kids could call to hear messages from cartoon characters or celebrities, often without realizing the cost.
12. **a)** Garbage Pail Kids
13. **c)** Reebok Pumps
14. **c)** Capri Sun
15. **a)** Creepy Crawlers
16. **a)** True – Kids were obsessed with collecting and trading stickers, with albums being a huge trend.
17. **b)** Strawberry Shortcake

18. **a)** Guess

19. **b)** Cupcake Surprise

20. **d)** Nintendo Entertainment System (NES)

ENTERTAINMENT & CULTURE

1. **b)** Top Gun
2. **b)** The Buggles
3. **a)** True – Shoulder pads were huge in '80s fashion, making outfits look powerful and structured.
4. **a)** Teddy Ruxpin
5. **a)** The Baby-Sitters Club
6. **b)** Alf
7. **a)** True – "Like a Virgin" reached number one in December 1984 and stayed there for six weeks.
8. **b)** Sixteen Candles
9. **c)** Tetris
10. **b)** "Where's the beef?"
11. **b)** False – The Sony Walkman was famous for playing cassette tapes, allowing people to take their music on the go.
12. **b)** Oprah Winfrey
13. **b)** „Thriller"
14. **c)** Darth Vader (Star Wars: The Empire Strikes Back)
15. **a)** Parachute pants
16. **b)** False – The "Macarena" was actually a '90s dance craze. The '80s had trends like the Moonwalk and the Running Man.
17. **b)** Harrison Ford
18. **a)** Donkey Kong
19. **a)** Michael Jackson
20. **a)** The A-Team

HISTORICAL EVENTS & HEADLINES

1. **b)** Ronald Reagan
2. **b)** Ukraine
3. **b)** False – The Berlin Wall fell in 1989.
4. **b)** Sandra Day O'Connor
5. **c)** 1986
6. **b)** Iran-Iraq War
7. **b)** False – The Tiananmen Square protests ended in a military crackdown with significant casualties.
8. **c)** Olympic Games
9. **b)** Margaret Thatcher
10. **a)** Black Monday
11. **a)** True – The 1980s saw the rise of affordable personal computers from companies like Apple, IBM, and Commodore.
12. **c)** Ronald Reagan
13. **b)** Exxon Valdez Oil Spill
14. **b)** Falkland Islands
15. **b)** Nelson Mandela
16. **b)** False – MTV launched in 1981 as a 24-hour music video channel, not a news channel.
17. **a)** United States
18. **b)** The People Power Revolution
19. **d)** Geneva Summit
20. **c)** HIV/AIDS Epidemic

TECHNOLOGY & INNOVATION

1. **b)** IBM PC
2. **b)** 1982
3. **b)** False – The first version of Microsoft Windows, Windows 1.0, was released in 1985.

4. **b)** Motorola DynaTAC 8000X
5. **b)** Fujifilm QuickSnap
6. **b)** Electronic fuel injection
7. **b)** False – The first laptop computer, the Osborne 1, was released in 1981, not by Apple.
8. **c)** The Challenger disaster
9. **b)** Sony
10. **c)** Mario
11. **a)** True – The Space Shuttle Columbia was launched on April 12, 1981.
12. **b)** Macintosh
13. **a)** The depletion of the ozone layer
14. **b)** Airfone
15. **c)** Nintendo Game Boy
16. **a)** True – The first GPS satellite was launched in 1989, forming the early foundation for global positioning systems.
17. **b)** DeLorean DMC-12
18. **b)** Ryanair
19. **b)** B-2 Spirit
20. **b)** The 1G cellular network

SPORTS & BIG ACHIEVEMENTS

1. **b)** Pittsburgh Steelers
2. **a)** Mike Tyson
3. **b)** False – The Soviet Union and Eastern Bloc nations boycotted the 1984 Los Angeles Olympics in response to the U.S. boycott of the 1980 Moscow Olympics.
4. **c)** United States
5. **b)** Larry Bird
6. **c)** Steffi Graf
7. **a)** True – The Chicago Bears won Super Bowl XX in January 1986, led by their famous defense and coach Mike Ditka.

8. a) San Francisco 49ers
9. a) Ben Johnson
10. b) Nick Faldo
11. a) True – Wayne Gretzky was traded to the Los Angeles Kings in 1988, shocking the hockey world.
12. b) Los Angeles Lakers
13. b) Sunday Silence
14. d) Mexico
15. a) True – Björn Borg retired from Grand Slam competition after the 1981 U.S. Open, making Wimbledon 1981 his last final against McEnroe.
16. a) New York Mets
17. c) Michael Jordan
18. c) Bernard Hinault
19. b) Eric Dickerson
20. a) Jose Canseco

The 1990s

DAILY LIFE & CHILDHOOD MEMORIES

1. a) Beanie Babies
2. b) Gel Pens
3. a) True – Goosebumps by R.L. Stine was a top-selling children's book series, becoming a major cultural phenomenon.
4. b) Green and black
5. c) Doc Martens
6. d) Tamagotchi
7. b) False – „One Sweet Day" by Mariah Carey & Boyz II Men held the record for the longest No. 1 run of the 1990s.
8. c) VHS tapes
9. c) Squeeze Pops
10. b) JNCO jeans

11. **b)** False – Lisa Frank's designs were primarily targeted at young girls with bright colors, unicorns, and rainbow themes.
12. **b)** Dunkaroos
13. **c)** Legends of the Hidden Temple
14. **b)** Snap bracelets
15. **b)** False – Boy Meets World was not a spin-off of Saved by the Bell, though both were popular '90s teen shows.
16. **b)** Skittles
17. **d)** Double Dare
18. **d)** Pager
19. **d)** Slam Book
20. **c)** Inflatable Chairs

ENTERTAINMENT & CULTURE

1. **c)** Beauty and the Beast
2. **a)** Seinfeld
3. **b)** False – Harry Potter and the Sorcerer's Stone was first published in the UK in 1997 under the title Harry Potter and the Philosopher's Stone.
4. **b)** The Macarena
5. **d)** Backstreet Boys
6. **b)** Friends
7. **b)** False – Those were their stage names; their real names were Victoria, Melanie C, Melanie B, Emma, and Geri.
8. **b)** Titanic
9. **c)** Nirvana
10. **b)** "Whassup?"
11. **b)** False – Will Smith had made appearances in music videos and TV specials before The Fresh Prince of Bel-Air.
12. **c)** Alanis Morissette
13. **b)** Baggy jeans
14. **c)** Johnny Depp
15. **b)** False – Tamagotchis were always intended as entertainment, not a learning tool.

16. **c)** The Real World
17. **c)** Eminem
18. **b)** Twin Peaks
19. **b)** South Park
20. **c)** The Lion King

HISTORICAL EVENTS & HEADLINES

1. **c)** The collapse of the Soviet Union
2. **a)** NAFTA
3. **a)** True – Nelson Mandela was elected president of South Africa in 1994, marking the end of apartheid.
4. **c)** O.J. Simpson
5. **c)** Rwanda
6. **b)** Euro
7. **a)** True – The World Trade Organization (WTO) was established in 1995 to regulate international trade.
8. **c)** The funeral of Princess Diana
9. **a)** Rodney King
10. **c)** Hong Kong
11. **a)** True – NATO intervened in Kosovo in 1999 to prevent ethnic cleansing by Serbian forces.
12. **b)** The Branch Davidians
13. **c)** The Kyoto Protocol
14. **c)** 1998
15. **b)** False – Despite widespread fear, the Y2K crisis did not cause significant failures, thanks to extensive software updates.
16. **c)** Madeleine Albright
17. **b)** The Oklahoma City bombing
18. **b)** Bill Clinton
19. **b)** False – Dolly the sheep was cloned in 1996 by Scottish scientists, but it was not a NASA project.
20. **c)** Iraq

TECHNOLOGY & INNOVATION

1. **c)** Mosaic
2. **c)** PlayStation
3. **a)** True – The first-ever text message („Merry Christmas") was sent in 1992.
4. **a)** MP3 player
5. **b)** Hotmail
6. **b)** Windows 95
7. **a)** True – Google was founded in 1998 by Larry Page and Sergey Brin.
8. **b)** EZ-Pass
9. **c)** Hubble Space Telescope
10. **b)** Amazon
11. **a)** True – DVDs were introduced in 1996, eventually replacing VHS as the primary home video format.
12. **a)** Game Boy Color
13. **a)** Beeper
14. **b)** False – The Mars Pathfinder was not the first spacecraft to reach another planet, but it was the first to successfully deploy a rover on Mars.
15. **b)** Intel
16. **c)** eBay
17. **b)** Capacitive touchscreens
18. **b)** Mars Climate Orbiter
19. **a)** True – Wi-Fi technology was introduced in 1997, with the first consumer devices appearing soon after.
20. **a)** Electronic Stability Control (ESC)

SPORTS & BIG ACHIEVEMENTS

1. **a)** United States
2. **b)** Tiger Woods
3. **b)** False – The 1992 „Dream Team" went undefeated, winning by an average of 44

points per game.

4. **c)** Chicago Bulls
5. **b)** Brandi Chastain
6. **c)** Denver Broncos
7. **a)** True – The 1994 MLB strike led to the cancellation of the World Series for the first time since 1904.
8. **c)** Michael Schumacher
9. **a)** Detroit Red Wings
10. **b)** Mike Tyson vs. Evander Holyfield
11. **a)** True – Manchester United defeated Bayern Munich 2-1 after scoring twice in stoppage time.
12. **a)** Michael Johnson
13. **c)** Tennessee
14. **b)** Lyn St. James
15. **a)** True – The 1994 FIFA World Cup Final ended in a penalty shootout, with Brazil defeating Italy.
16. **a)** Pete Sampras
17. **a)** Serena Williams
18. **a)** Mark McGwire
19. **b)** Magic Johnson
20. **b)** False – Baseball was included in the 1996 Olympics, but professional players were not allowed to compete until the 2000 Olympics.

FEEDBACK

Thank you for choosing Nostalgic Trivia for Seniors! We hope it brings back fond memories and a touch of the past to your day.

We Value Your Feedback

Your insights help us improve and create books you love. If you're enjoying this trivia book, please consider leaving a short review on Amazon. It takes just 20 seconds, but your feedback is invaluable to us and helps future customers too.

Here's How to Leave a Review:

1. *Log in to your Amazon account.*
2. *Find „Nostalgic Trivia for Seniors".*
3. *Share what you enjoyed most!*

If you have any suggestions for improvement, you can scan this QR code. It will take you to a form where you can easily share your ideas with us.

Thank you and enjoy your cozy trip down memory lane!

CHECK OUT OUR WORD SEARCH SERIES

Today!

Printed in Dunstable, United Kingdom

76789705R00131